MINA`S MOU

MINA`S

MOUNTAIN

by

Evelyn Julia Kent

based on
the true story of Hermione Bohm

Published in 1997
by
Evelyn Julia Kent Associates
7 Savernake Court, Stanmore, England. HA7 2RA

Printed and bound in Great Britain by
Antony Rowe Ltd., Chippenham, Wiltshire.

ISBN 0 9523716 69

A CIP Catalogue record for this book
is available from the British Library

Author's note: This is a true story. As it has been told to the author
from memory, some of the names and incidental details may not be
accurate.

Dedicated to the memory of
Fay Kramer

To everything there is a season
and a time to every purpose under the heaven:
A time to be born, and a time to die;
A time to plant, and a time to reap;
A time to kill, and a time to heal;
A time to break down, and a time to build up;
A time to weep, and a time to laugh;
A time to mourn, and a time to dance:

(from Ecclesiastes 3)

CONTENTS

FINALE: *(1945-1947)*

Photograph of Hermione and Josef Bohm on their wedding day.

Epilogue

Historical background to events in the story

Acknowledgements

I wish to thank all those who have generously given their time and talents to the production of this book, especially to Moira Poley, whose kindness, patience and computer expertise enabled the story to get into print.

I am indebted to Fay Marks for her watercolour of the mountain, Dachstein, and to Roz Moradian for the sillhouettes on the front cover. Special thanks to Maurice Kanarek for all his work on the final design; to my colleague Michael Davies, for his scholarly historical notes of the times against which the story is set; to Bobby Marks for proof-reading and to John O'Toole for his sympathetic editing. My appreciation goes to Bodo Klingenberg for translating from German and for giving the writer another viewpoint. I am indebted to Terry Charman, Senior Historical Researcher at the Imperial War Museum, for his interest and knowledge in verifying certain details.

Particular thanks are due to Frank Entwistle, whose wisdom and support were invaluable.

Finally, my love and thanks go to Hermione Bohm, whose recollections have been the basis of *Mina's Mountain*.

MINA`S MOUNTAIN

PART ONE

Peace
(1919 - 1938)

1 FATHER

I have lived many years.   Many more than my tall, good-looking father, who owned a farm in the Austrian mountains.   My warm-hearted mother worked alongside him, when she was not having babies.

I was born on the 18th April, 1919, in their farmhouse set high on a hilltop overlooking the village of Neustift, in the area of Steiermark. I was the baby, with three older brothers and two older sisters, until Hedwig came along four years later. So I was number six.

By 1923 there were seven of us enjoying the warm summers together, helping on the farm, taking on daily tasks. Of course, we spent a lot of time just rolling about in haystacks and screaming with delight as we jumped into the farm reservoir to swim around with the fish. Then, every day   was wonderful because the world was at peace.

In the valley,   church bells rang out every Sunday. During the first May of my life, when baby chicks pecked in the yard and calves nudged the udders of cows for warm, sweet milk, while the apple and pear blossoms floated gently in the air from our orchards, my father carried me down the dry farm track to the village church to be christened *Hermione.*

The whole family followed happily behind Father. Franz and Alois tried to out-step each other on the way down. Maria and Josephine skipped along beside Mother, who held onto Joseph, because he was still only two years old.

"Say *Hermione*," said Maria laughingly to Joseph.

"Mee, Mina," Joseph managed obligingly. So that became my name in the family.

The seasons changed slowly on the farm, regulating work as the year tumbled out, month after month. Springtime brought hope of new life. But there was ceaseless toil in summer promising full storehouses by autumn, if we were lucky.

Everything on our farm was recycled, the cow manure, the pig manure, chicken manure, even ours. Our toilet was in a pretty little hut away from the farmhouse. It had a shiny wooden seat, and if I sat there quietly for a while I could hear tiny creatures scrabbling about outside. Every so often, when it was full, Father would empty the contents over the land while we ran away holding our noses. But this activity kept the land so fertile that Father could get at least two crops a year from his fields. First corn, then oats. First vegetables, then wheat. First grazing, then potatoes.

Rotating crops on the land every year like this produced enough for us all and more besides to sell.

By the late summer of 1923, I was a sturdy little girl of four trying my best to keep up with my older brothers and sisters who milked the cows, moved the oxen to pasture, fed the pigs and chickens, searched for eggs in special hiding places.

"Let me help. I want to help," I insisted, trying to show I was much more grown-up than everyone thought.

"Come along then," said Father. He lifted me on to his shoulders and encouraged me to pick the best cherries from the highest branches. Franz and Joseph scrambled up other fruit trees, knocking down unripe apples, which made Father mad.

I remember helping with the harvest for the first time that year. I felt it was important to assist my father and brothers in the fields. We returned home one evening, exhausted but happy. Strangely, Mother was not in the kitchen as usual. We called out for her.

"I'm here," she answered, from her bedroom.

I was astonished to find her lying in bed. Even more surprised to see a baby in my Mother's arms.

"You're such a big girl now," said Mother, smiling at me. "You will be able to help me out with your new sister."

So little Hedwig became my first charge.

When the first snowflakes drifted down to cover the fields and outhouses, smoothing mud paths and timber stacks, we put the farm animals safely in barns. The stone stove in the kitchen-living room devoured our wood stocks in winter, but it kept us snug against the howling winds outside. Every Friday, Mother would bake bread for the week. At Christmas time, the smell of extra cakes and pudding enhanced our sense of well-being. Nothing frightened us. We were safe in our farmhouse.

By December, the farm road had become waist high in snow. A serene silence pervaded the valley and crept up the hillside so that we felt wrapped around by God's goodness. We waited eagerly for the magical moment when He was born in a manger, bringing peace and goodwill to all mankind.

The little church glowed with a hundred candles as my family trudged through the snow for Midnight Mass. Villagers greeted each other as they pressed together to keep warm and listen to the choir.   The music swelled, filling our hearts.   When a choir boy sang his solo, Mother said "It takes me back to the good old days" and dabbed her eyes with her handkerchief.

I knew the story of the Nativity by heart. How a bright star led wise men to Bethlehem.

"Can stars really show the way?" I asked Maria.

"Sailors use them as maps," she said knowingly.   "They pinpoint the sky to learn which way to go. If you look at the night sky, I'll show you the plough. Then if you follow the line of the top two stars it will point to the North star."

"Do you think stars are where angels live?"   I wanted to know, but Maria was not certain.

I truly believed in angels. I loved to hear how they had appeared to shepherds, out on the hillside beyond Bethlehem, especially to tell them the good news that a saviour had been born to bring peace to the world. How the shepherds had gone into town and found the baby safely in a barn, just like ours, amongst all the farm animals. It had all happened such a long time ago, and yet it seemed to be happening at the very moment we were in the church, looking at the crib, being carried along by the music.

We joined in singing *Stille Nacht, Heilige Nacht, Alles schlaft, einer wacht. (Silent Night, Holy Night).*

I snuggled up to Hedwig in bed that special night, listening to the night owls and hoping for a gift from Santa Klaus. Mother had tied pretty coloured parcels of sugar lumps and small, white candles to a fir tree that Father had brought in from the forest. All my brothers and sisters were home for Christmas-time. The family was complete and contented.

The following year, the harvest looked good. Ripened corn lay on the slopes surrounding the farmhouse, waiting to be gathered in. Everyone was involved. Even neighbours came to help feed the large threshing-machine. We watched it gobble up corn stalks at one end and spew out grains to mill into flour at the other. There was more than enough for a year's bread.

"Run to the farmhouse," Father told me, "and tell your Mother to bring up some food and drink. We're almost through and I want to share our good fortune with everybody."

I skipped along towards the kitchen where Mother (with Hedwig trying to assist!) was making delicious sandwiches and drinks for all the helpers.

Suddenly I could hear screams and shouting coming from the field. Franz came racing past me yelling for Mother. Several neighbours followed after him on their way down to the village to fetch the priest.

By nightfall, we knew that our happy days were over. Father had taken a bad fall when part of the threshing machine collapsed with him on top. His head had banged against the ground, his body skewed under him, and he had broken his neck and died.

I cried myself to sleep. All of us were numb with the tragedy. None of us ever imagined such a terrible thing would happen. On the day of the funeral, it was a sad little procession that followed his coffin down the hillside to the cemetery.

Somehow, Mother pulled on her inner strength and encouraged us to look forward.

"Our harvest is home. The barns are full. Father has seen to it that we will not starve this winter... we must be brave and carry on as best we can."

I placed a posy of wild flowers on Father's grave and sighed. Next spring seemed a long way away.

2 CONFESSION

Christmas was a sad time. The snow fell heavily all night. None of us went to Midnight Mass. We all knew there would be no gifts from Santa Klaus. Mother cried herself to sleep often. This night Maria crept into her bedroom and into her bed to comfort her.

The winter was bleak, made harder by Father's absence. More and more tasks fell to the older children, especially Alois, Franz and Joseph. Work on the farm was excessively hard, more so for a woman on her own trying to raise a family. Despite all our efforts to help, Mother knew she would have to re-marry simply to keep the farm going.

One Sunday in early spring, Mother came home with a tall, thin farmer.

"He is your new father," she told us.

We were quite put out.

"Just call me Joseph," said the young man, smiling.

"I'm Joseph!" retorted our Joseph, rudely.

"Well, I'll be Big Joseph then. Big Joe, how's that?"

We all laughed and immediately became friends. Mother smiled quietly to herself, then bustled about to fetch a special apple-cake which she served with cider, so we could all celebrate her marriage. Big Joe was younger than Mother, but they seemed contented with each other.

The hard work of the farm continued throughout that year, with good crops and healthy farm animals keeping us well fed and busy.

While I was helping to toss the hay for drying, the thought of Father came deep into my mind. I liked Big Joe, but I knew no-one could take the place of my soft-hearted Father. Tears welled up and I could not stop crying. Maria came and put her arm around me.

"I know you're sad for Father," she said. " But even though he is not here, I'm sure he watches over us with Jesus. So we must do our best for him, mustn't we?"

I hugged Maria tightly. She was a dear sister who always seemed to understand me.

"Cheer up!" she went on. "You're starting at the village school next week. Won't that be fun?"

And it was, except that I came home with nits and Mother had to wash my hair with paraffin. When I returned to school everyone complained that I smelt, but the teacher stood up for me saying "If your mothers had looked after you as well as Mina's, then she would not have caught your nits!"

I could already read because Maria had helped me, and I loved learning new things. We did reading, drawing, needlework, history, geography, singing and lots of maths.

The more I went to school, the better I liked it. Father Peter, the priest, came to teach us our catechism which we had to learn off by heart. *I believe in God the Father, God the Son and God the Holy Ghost.... And Jesus Christ, His only Son, Our Lord...*

One morning, he took the class into the Church and showed us the Confessional. It was a tiny box-room, like an upright coffin, with a little seat and a funny little grated window.

"Now, when you say your confession," he told us seriously, "remember that Guardian Angels are watching over you and can see all you do."

My mouth dropped open. The thought of an angel watching me pee was very unsettling. When I next went to our little toilet house, I had a good look all around outside first, and then inside, to make sure I was on my own.

"Father, bless me 'cause I have sinned," I gasped, on my first confession. I could see Father Peter's nose on the other side of the little window.

"My child, tell me ..."

"I swore. I said *shit!* when the cow kicked me. Then I pulled Josephine's plaits. I didn't want to help Alois with the pigs, or Joseph with the horses. And then I spilt the flour bag all over the floor so that Mother hit me ."

"Come, come, all is forgiven."   I could hear him chuckling. "You know, everyone gets angry and upset sometimes. Everybody makes mistakes.. and you can be sure that accidents happen now and then that make you mad. But everything comes out well in the end."

"Does it, Father?"

"You have to be patient child."

"I want to confess something else, Father."

He sighed behind the grating. "You don't have to tell me any more. I was young once. You only need to tell me one or two."

But I could not stop. All the thoughts that I had kept inside me wanted to come tumbling out. Here at last was somebody who listened.

"I hate getting up early to work on the farm. Sometimes I just want to do nothing at all except lie in the fields and look at the sky. Someone is always ordering me about. I feel like a slave!"

"We are all on God's earth to help each other. Now run along. And recite one *Hail Mary* for your sins ...*such as they are!*"

Back in the classroom, Herr Yamenek was reading a story from the Brothers Grimm. It was about a little match girl, cold and alone, with nothing to console her. I suddenly realised how lucky I was to have a loving family with dear brothers and sisters. I resolved to make the best of it for the time being.

In the warm sunlight of autumn, I trudged back along the dusty track to the farmhouse, feeling the weight of the metal rucksack filled with buttermilk on my back. Now that my elder brothers and sister, Alois, Franz and Maria, no longer went to the village school each morning, I had to help to take the daily quota of milk down into the valley. Here it was made into butter and cheese and the buttermilk returned in the evening to feed our animals. The weight never varied, it was always a heavy burden. But today my spirits lifted as I walked the mile back clutching a book that Herr Yamenek had allowed me to borrow.

"I have a story book to read!" I exclaimed in the kitchen, as I tipped the rucksack off my shoulder.

Mother was kneading and pounding dough before leaving it in a basin to rise. The fire under the stone stove blazed; glowing embers would soon heat the oven cupboard ready to bake enough bread for the coming week.

"You know you have work to do yet, Mina." She wiped her forehead with the back of her hand and sighed.

I sighed too. The cows needed to graze along the grass verges of the fields. Hedwig and I had to take their tethers and lead them out.

"New crunchy apples to eat!" Mother encouraged us. "You can pick some from the orchard as you pass by."

"Work on a farm never ceases, not for one minute," I thought grudgingly. I set off with the tethers in one hand and `Snow White` in the other. Docile cows ambled from their barn, happy to be let out to graze on the luscious pasture of the hillside. Hedwig skipped behind waving her stick.

As we walked along the mud lane I managed to open my book. The words were written in large print and there were some pages with illustrations. The story itself enchanted me. I became Snow White wandering in the forest. I saw little creatures around my feet. Some day *my* prince would come. But Big Joe , my kindly step-father, would never chase *me* out. My adventures would start when I was much older. We found a suitable spot in the meadow-land to throw ourselves down.

"You want to know what I think, Hedwig?"

Her mouth was full of juicy white apple pulp so she nodded her head.

"I think fairy tales do come true. Even if bad things happen, everything is for the best. Anyway, Father Peter said so."

"What bad things?" Hedwig chewed on the apple core.

"Nothing, I was just thinking." I closed the book. " It won`t always be summertime, will it?"

3 MOTHER

By mid-winter, the haylofts were filled with sweet-smelling hay. Sacks of potatoes, parsnips and carrots lay stored in the cellar. The flour jars were full. Preserves of cherry jam and chutney stood on shelves. Sides of bacon and ham hung from their hooks. Cider matured in barrels. Sausage-worsht was strung from the rafters. The aroma of a large Christmas pudding permeated the farmhouse. Soup bubbled in the huge black cauldron and pork was roasting in the oven.

We went to Midnight Mass on Christmas Eve with Mother and Big Joe. We all felt secure and happy to be together for Christmas. The snow crunched under our feet as we walked on top of it. Everything lay serene in the moonlight.

On Christmas morning, Mother and I milked the cows a little later than usual. Snow sparkled along the lane as I took the daily quota of milk down to the dairy. Everyone in the village cheerily wished me 'Merry Christmas'. The church bell chimed merrily as I peeped into the chantry. Baby Jesus lay smiling in His crib surrounded by the same docile animals that I tended every day. Mary and Joseph, looking very much like my older brother and sister, watched over their charge. Father Peter bustled in and beamed at me.

17

"Our blessed Saviour is born, bringing peace to the world," he said. "Isn't that something to praise the Lord for?"

In the early evening, after Big Joe had made sure everything was battened down against the storms, when all the farm jobs were completed, we sat round the large wooden table to enjoy our meal. It was rare for us all to be together. The older girls, Maria and Josephine lived away from home in large mansions, because they had to earn their own living as housemaids. Franz helped run a farm in another valley and led an independent life. There was more than enough to eat and plenty of cider to drink. We could hear the wind outside beginning to whip against the trees and the soft neighing of shire-horses in their stable.

"I had better go to check the horses," Big Joe said, rising from the table. A gust of chill air streaked across the kitchen as the wooden door slammed behind him. He seemed to be gone for ages.

"Joseph, see if Joe is having difficulty securing the barn doors," said Mother, dishing out second helpings of pudding.

Joseph was gone for ages as well.

"Something is wrong," murmured Mother. She left the table to look out of the door. Joe was staggering across the yard, his arm slung around Joseph's shoulder.

"What is it? What's happened?" screamed Mother as she helped them inside.

"Nothing, nothing." Big Joe sank into his chair. "Just a touch of cramp," he gasped. "Get me some hot water."

I grabbed the kettle from the hob and poured hot water into a mug. He sipped it, while we all stood around anxiously watching his white face.

"Too much good food, I expect. It's nothing," he repeated.

But it was not nothing. He lost weight rapidly over the next few weeks. By spring the doctors had diagnosed a stomach tumour and we knew he had not much time left to live. Mother nursed him tenderly.

Meanwhile, the farm work was getting behind. Spring sowing had to be done; there was the never-ending work of tending to cattle, horses, pigs and chickens, quite apart from bills waiting to be paid. Alois and Joseph stayed away from school to run the farm as best they could. I helped as much as I was able to. Mother showed me how to bake bread and the weekly task of making the loaves became mine.

In early Summer, Big Joe sank into a coma and died, leaving Mother bereft and heartbroken. Father Peter organised neighbours in the village to take turns in helping us. Somehow the farm continued to run well enough to feed us.

Maria, Josephine and Franz all managed to send home a little money. But we were terribly poor and had hardly enough for any extras, like sugar. Mother was desperate, wondering how to make ends meet. She became very bad-tempered and hit us for even the smallest thing. It seemed that life on our farm was draining her of every bit of energy and humour. She sobbed into her apron that she did not even have enough money for the kitchen basics, not even salt or pepper.

It was a warm summer, and by September the hedgerows were bending with hips and cobnuts. One weekend, Joseph nailed up a little cart from a wooden box and four old pram wheels.

"The brambles are heavy with blackberries," he said. "Why don't you and Hedwig take the cart into the forest and see what you can gather?"

We trundled the cart along ancient pathways that led to the Baron's castle deep in the forest. Every now and then we came upon a clearing edged with high, rambling brambles, where we spent hours picking luscious blackberries. Our pigtails caught in the prickles, our hands were dark stained from the juices, our skirts ripped on the undergrowth, but we were engrossed and happy. There were more than enough blackberries to fill our cart to the brim. We would come again tomorrow for cranberries and nuts. We pulled the cart happily behind us heading home past the castle walls. As we neared the entrance, a little old lady, tapping a walking stick, came to the gates and looked out at us. I recognised her as the old Baroness who distributed charity in the village from time to time.

"You children have been busy," she said, smiling at us.

Behind her appeared her tall, ugly son. We stood dumb and frightened as he strode towards us waving his riding crop.

"Hey! You children!" yelled the Baron. "Where have you been picking those berries?"

"In the woods," I said, pointing to the forest around us.

"These are my woods - my forest. You are stealing!" he roared.

"Anyone can have berries!" I shouted back. "And I am not a thief!"

The old Baroness rocked with laughter. We could hear her chiding her son as we ran away as fast as we could, dragging the cart behind us.
It was a good crop. Mother was delighted.

"Take them to the village shop. See what you can get for them," she said.

That evening, Hedwig and I brought home sugar, tea and coffee, all bought with money earned from the blackberries. It cheered Mother up. We felt we had contributed something worthwhile to the family store. But we all realised that the farm was too much for one woman and her children. It needed a strong man to run it, to repair the outhouses, plough the oxen, kill the pigs.

Wigel was headman on a neighbouring farm. He was tall, strong and kindly. If he married Mother he would take on the responsibility of running our farm and own a half share. It was decided that they should wed after harvest.

Once again, Mother went to the altar. This time she had Franz, Alois, Joseph, Maria, Hedwig and myself beside her. This time she wore a simple summer dress and cried when they made their vows *Till death us do part.* Father Peter blessed the union and all the village turned out to wish them well.

Everyone felt this marriage was right for both of them. I was just seven years old and this was my third father. I liked him. He was very kindly, he never grumbled at us. I prayed to Jesus that night that this time it would be forever.

4 JOSEPH

(*Winter 1926*)

My brother, Joseph, was the one I loved best of all. He was nearly three years older but we shared many jobs around the farm. We both carried metal rucksacks, filled with the morning's milk, down to the dairy on our way to school. When the weather was fine, we tramped along together, talking of everything under the sun. When winter snow and ice made the mud tracks almost impassable, we skied down, exhilarated by the speed and movement of our bodies. We were good companions. So I was dismayed when I overheard Wigel and Mother discussing his future.

"I'm around now to do the man's jobs," said Wigel. "Alois is a great help here and neighbours give extra hands at harvest-time."

"Soon we shall have another mouth to feed. We hardly have enough money to go round as it is," said Mother, disconsolately. "Yes. I think it is time for Joseph to leave. He is old enough to earn his own living."

(*1927*)

I sobbed my heart out in Springtime when Joseph packed his meagre belongings and set off. He was to be a farm-hand on a smallholding the other side of the mountains. He seemed quite happy.

"Cheer up, Mina. I`m eleven. Grown up enough to work for my keep."

"I want to come with you."

He laughed at me.

"Will you come with me all my life? When I marry?"

"Of course not, silly!"

"Well, then. Stay here and enjoy the Summer," he grinned. "You are the oldest girl at home now - so you are going to be busy."

I certainly was. Wigel took over the main share of the farmwork, helped by Alois. By now, Hedwig was three and, quite apart from all the other things I had to do, she was in my care. There was more than enough work for Mother, who was expecting her eighth child. I had less time than ever at school, which upset me. Herr Yamenek was very understanding when I was absent for days on end. On the windowsill in our farmhouse were some second-hand school books, which I took out to read as often as I could.

"What is the capital of France?" he asked the class during a Geography lesson.

My hand shot up.

"Hermione Kohl, you wouldn`t know this," he said, kindly. "You have to work too hard at home."

"I do know," I replied indignantly.

"Tell me."

"It`s Paris."

"I know where you got that from. You`ve been minding the cows!"

Everybody in the class laughed at me, but he was right. I had studied our little atlas carefully in the fields.

"And what is the capital of England?" he questioned.

Hands shot up, but I shouted out first, "London - and I am going there one day!"

He roared with laughter and all the class yelled `English!` at me.

When I arrived home that evening, a new baby sister had arrived. Hedwig was screaming her head off because no one had had time for her. I made the evening meal for the men and Mother, and placated Hedwig with a piece of apple-cake.

As I grew, I loved taking part in sports at school with my playmates. We ran along the mud lanes, swam in the cool river, played football. I was good in goal. I entered into every new activity enthusiastically. I could read and write well. I learnt shorthand and arithmetic, history and geography.

I could sew and knit well enough to make clothes for my younger sisters. I sang in the church choir. I could ski downhill faster than anyone else in my class. Every day was filled with farmwork,schoolwork and housework. Never an hour to myself!

But Sunday was a quiet space in the week to take a breath and be thankful to be alive. I still had to deliver the milk quota to the dairy, but I went into Sunday school after that, happy to listen to bible stories and learn new hymns to sing in the choir. It was as though I drew energy from being in God`s house.

My Sunday school teacher was called Alphana. She was the youngest daughter of a local farm-owner. She was tall, very beautiful and extremely kindly. She often walked back with me to our farm to call in on Mother and the baby. I was certain she would make a good match and become a lady in a grand house. To my astonishment, one Sunday she told us she was hoping to go away to become a Novice.

"Who will teach us catechism?" I cried.

"Father Peter will still be here. I will visit from time to time."

"But I shall miss you!"

"Mina, do something special for me," she said, confidentially. "Learn your lessons well and your catechism and when you are confirmed - I will be your godmother. Would you like that?"

It seemed wonderful that such a beautiful and serene person could care for me. I vowed to do my best for her.

(Autumn 1929)

Although Wigel and Mother worked as hard as ever, the farm never seemed to bring in enough money. We were always hard up. Mother continually grumbled at Wigel, or hit out at me for the slightest thing.

Before the snows came, Joseph paid us one of his rare visits. He looked fit and tall. He came with a letter from Frau Spritzer, his employer. Her housemaid was leaving to get married and she wanted Mother to find someone from the village to help with her two young children and do the housework.

"You can go, Mina." Mother nodded at me. "That way we won't have to feed you, and you can earn a little money."

"Mother!" I protested. "Who will look after you and baby Anna?"

"Hedwig is growing up. She can help out now."

So it was settled.

I set off over the mountains by Joseph's side, happy to be with him once more, but wondering what was in store.

Herr and Frau Spritzer were very surprised when when Joseph announced that I was their new housemaid.

"But she can't be more than ten years old!" exclaimed Frau Spritzer.

"Don't worry," said Joseph, with absolute faith. "She can do everything!"

That was how it turned out to be. Every day I fed their fourteen cows, brushed and washed them down, milked them, cleaned the cowshed. They were such docile, gentle creatures. They needed me to look after them. Afterwards, I fed the chickens, collected eggs from their hidden nests, cleaned their coops.

When that was done, I cleaned the kitchen, raked the fire, gathered logs to stoke the oven. I did the washing. Then on Fridays I had to knead the dough and make enough loaves to last the week. I made almond cakes and currant buns. I cooked the meals and fed the children. Every evening, when I put them to bed, they listened enraptured as I read stories or told them fairy tales. Then I fell exhausted into my own bed. Before I knew it the night was over and another day dawned.

It was the night before Christmas. The little crucifix on my attic bedroom wall glowed in the moonlight. There would be no gifts this year, but I thought I could give my cows a treat. In the early hours, I crept out to the hayloft, up the ladder and pitched an extra bale over the top for my animals . Suddenly, a hand caught hold of me and pulled me down into the straw.

"Let me go!" I squealed.

"What are you doing?" Joseph peered at me in the dawn light.

"What are *you* doing?" I spluttered.

"Pinching extra food for my horses."

"So am I, for my cows," I giggled.

We both fell about laughing that we had the same idea of giving our charges extra Christmas dinner.

Joseph tended his four shire horses while I milked the cows and fed them well. We made sure the barn doors were secure against the buffeting winds which were beginning to drive snow down in drifts. Joseph and I had decided we would walk the five miles home that afternoon to see our family, but by mid-morning everything was shrouded under mounds of snow and the farmhouse was completely isolated.

Inside was cosy and warm. Frau Spritzer had decorated the fir tree in the   corner of the room most prettily, with tiny white crochet stars, coloured knitted socks and mittens, little painted wooden toys and coloured candles. She was a frail lady, who was often unwell, but she seemed to enjoy making everything feel festive. Herr Spritzer carved roast pork and crackling.

I handed round the plates. The cider jugs were soon emptied. We were feeling merry with food and drink. Although it was my first Christmas away from home, I was content that Joseph was with me. The Spritzer family made us feel very welcome.

Frau Spritzer followed me into the kitchen when I was clearing away.

"You are such a good help," she said, pressing my hand. "You`re a strong girl, you`re never ill," she added, wistfully.

"I haven`t time to be ill," I retorted, scornfully.

"Would you stay with us next year?" she continued.

I thought she meant me to come to visit next Christmas.

"I missed Midnight Mass and singing in the choir this year. I do miss lessons in school as well," I blurted out.

She nodded. "Ah, you don`t want to be a housemaid, you want to learn. I understand. You want to be more than a farmer`s wife." She sounded sad. "When the snows go, you can return to your village."

Joseph took me home in early spring. I was happy to leave. In my pocket was more money that I had ever had - thirty Austrian schillings. I had worked from five in the morning to nine every night for the past three months, non-stop, and earned ten schillings a month.

Wigel waved to us from the fields as we passed. Mother was baking and hugged me tightly against her floured apron. Hedwig jumped up and down wanting me to tell her everything. Alois and Joseph went off to chat. Anna cried for attention.

"I'll pick her up," I offered, going towards her cot, but Hedwig pushed me aside.

"No, that's my job," she said, rocking her little sister back to sleep.

I offered my money to Mother, but to my surprise she said, "You keep it."

"I don't mind if you need it," I said.

"No, dear. I know from Joseph that you've earned it. Buy something for yourself."

I could not wait to go down to the village shop. There I bought bleached linen, needles and thread, a small length of lace and strong elastic. I sat up all night making myself a petticoat and a pair of knickers to match.

"This will be for my confirmation day," I decided.

5 CONFIRMATION

(1930)

I returned happily to school. Father Peter told us that we were now in the confirmation class. We would have to work specially hard to be ready for the service in the spring. Some boys pulled faces, but most of us were excited to be the chosen group.

On Sunday morning, I hurried into church to find Alphana and tell her my news, but she was not there. Frau Yemenek took Sunday school that day.

"Alphana has left Neustift to become a novice," she told me.

"Where?" I was dismayed. "She promised to be my godmother at my confirmation."

"She is at the convent in Graz. She is going to be a nun," said Frau Yemenek proudly.

I had seen nuns wearing deep blue habits, starched white, winged hoods around serene, smiling faces. Suddenly, I wanted to be a nun too. I wanted to devote my life to Jesus and help people.

That night I talked to my crucifix and told Jesus what I had decided. Through the wall I could hear Mother and Wigel quarrelling. Mother shouting that we never had enough money, that she was tired of scrimping together. Nothing was calm or serene in our home.

On an organic farm like ours, we relied heavily upon the seasons. Throughout that year the weather had been uncertain and some of the crops had failed. For the first time I could remember, there was not enough food to feed us all. I had grown when I was away. Now I had to wear hand-down clothes left by Maria. She was much taller than me and I had to turn up the hems to prevent me looking like an old lady. My shoes did not fit any more, but since we did not wear shoes once the snows melted, I made do without them.

For my special day, I would have to cut the uppers of my old shoes to make more room. I tried them on. Hedwig laughed at my toes sticking out. I hugged her in bed that night.

"I`m Cinderella," I told her. "Just waiting for the right pair of shoes!"

We could hear constant rowing in the bedroom next door. Wigel was silent more often than not whilst Mother railed against him, as if it was his fault that nature had failed us.

"You`ll have to move out," Mother said to me eventually. "I just do not have enough to go round any more."

"But where?" I envisaged returning to the Spritzer household.

"I'll ask around," Mother said. "Someone is sure to want extra help."

"I shall miss classes," I protested.

"You want to eat, don't you?" she retorted, briskly.

After two weeks of asking around, I was told that a farmer wanted me for six months. He needed extra help. The small holding was not so far away as the Spritzer's household. I would be able to get back to Sunday school, at least. I made up my mind that it was for the best. Anyway, I would earn enough money to make myself a white confirmation dress. It was something to look forward to.

Alone in a tiny, cold bedroom, I set my crucifix on the wall. This was not what I expected. Instead of the warmth of the Spritzer household, the farmer and his wife were acidly cold to me. They needed me as a farmhand, cleaning out stables, digging and planting fields, doing all the heavy work on the land.

At mealtimes I was ravenous, but whilst they piled their plates high, my portions were meagre. I was made to eat alone. I was always hungry. I truly felt like Cinderella and prayed my fairy godmother would appear to save me, but she did not.

Father Peter voiced his concern when he saw me before Confession.

"Are you well, my child?"

"Yes, Father."

"You look very thin. Do they feed you properly?"

He guessed the truth.

"Shall I speak to your parents?"

"No!" I did not dare tell Mother because she would have scolded me for being lazy and not earning my keep. But the truth was that the farmer and his wife were so mean that they treated me as slave labour.

The icy November winds chilled me to the bone. I wore large farmers' boots and several woollen jumpers to try to keep warm. I had no one to talk to, and only hard farm work to keep me occupied. At night I prayed to Jesus, suffering on the cross, to let me leave.

Three weeks before Christmas, when the snow was already a foot deep, I heard the neighing of a horse outside the barn. The huge doors creaked as I looked out to see Wigel dismounting from one of our horses.

"What's happened?" I cried, running to hug him.

"Mother has had a miscarriage. We need you home."

I started to cry, mostly with relief. He put his strong arm around my shoulder.

"Come along, Mina. Make your farewells here."

I packed my small bag with the little I owned and left, riding the horse with Wigel. Only on the way down into our valley did I realise that even though I had done my best, the farmer and his wife had not given me one penny for all the work I had done.

(Whitsun 1931)

The cockerel woke me as usual. Hedwig lay sleeping beside me taking in smooth, deep breaths. I left the bed quietly and went to the window. The air was warm and mild. The early morning sun was shining, making the green fields look like bright velvet cushions. All along the lane, apple and pear blossoms opened their petals to entice the bees. Pigeons cooed in the lofts. I could hear the soft lowing of cows in the barn. Away in the distance a church bell chimed. At long last, the day of my confirmation had arrived.

Before breakfast, Sister Alphana,my godmother, appeared at our farm. She knew my Mother from when they were school-friends and they greeted each other fondly. We ate breakfast of potato soup and thickly buttered bread.

Whilst Mother chatted to Sister Alphana, I went to change into my confirmation dress. It was not mine, of course. I had not been able to afford one. Mother had borrowed it from another friend whose daughter had been confirmed last year. It was a long, white cotton shift, with a lace yoke, collar and cuffs. It was miles too wide for me, so I tied my sash around it twice to pull it in. I wore my linen petticoat and knickers underneath. Mother lent me white stockings. On my feet, a gift from Wigel, were a pair of pigskin shoes large enough to last another year.

"You look like a bride!" exclaimed Hedwig.

"She will when she wears her headband," said Mother, pinning onto my flaxen hair an Alice band with flowers and a little white veil attached.

"My gift for you," offered Sister Alphana.

She held out a tissue paper package. As I undid it, I saw an ivory cross attached to a silver chain with black and white beads.

"My own rosary! Thank you," I breathed.

"Tie it to your sash. Make sure you don't lose it on the way," advised Mother.

Sister Alphana and I set off to walk the ten miles to the cathedral. On the way we joined other members of my class. By the time we neared the town we were a large crocodile of boys and girls, all clothed in white, all looking like angels.

We were ushered into our places and the service began. Each of us carried a white bible and a rosary in one hand, and held a lighted candle in the other. We walked sedately down the aisle to the singing of the choir and the resonant organ music.

Et dominus, filius et spiritus sancti.

The bishop made the sign of the cross on my forehead as I knelt to kiss the ring on his finger. I felt very grown-up when I took the sacrament.

Father Peter beamed at us from the pews as we turned to sit in our places to listen to the sermon.

"Dedicate yourselves to God. Dedicate yourselves to doing good. Dedicate yourselves to Jesus for the rest of your lives."

I would. I was ready and willing, thrilled to be touched by the Holy Spirit. I aspired to be a good Christian - maybe even a nun. My soul and spirit were being nourished. I felt quite faint with the enormity of it all.

After the service, we were taken to a local hotel, where frankfurters and potatoes, biscuits and cakes were handed out. Having food inside me made all the difference; the dizziness went and I felt replete in every way. That night, when I arrived home, tired but happy, I lay in bed cuddling Hedwig and thinking how lucky I was.

6 THE CONVENT

I worked harder than ever at the village school and took my exams when I was fourteen. I did very well, but where was I going to work now?

At the end of the school year, Mother received a letter from my godmother, Sister Alphana, suggesting I go to her convent in the city to continue my schooling.

"How can I possibly go to her convent school?" I moaned. "We are much too poor."

"I believe she has arranged something," said Mother, scanning the letter.

"Anyway, she will be in the valley, Ebersdorf, near here to visit at the end of August. You will be able to speak to her yourself."

"Would you be willing to work for your education?" Sister Alphana asked when we were together.

"I always do my school work when I can," I assured her.

"It is arranged that you can come to the convent school, so long as you help out in the kitchens."

"I can do that!" I exclaimed.

It was with great excitement that I travelled with my godmother to her convent in Graz. The building was far grander than I had imagined. Indeed, it was not only a convent and a select boarding school, it also housed a huge teaching hospital. The atmosphere was one of bustling efficiency and learning.

Sister took me to a small, neat bedroom in the nuns` quarters.

"This is your own room," she said. "That way you can be private and have your own time."

She smiled at me. "When you are ready, come down the back stairs, along the passage and meet me in the main hallway."

I unpacked my few belongings. I laid my rosary and white bible on top of the chest of drawers on the crochet cloth that my sister, Maria, had made especially for me.

I bounced up and down on the quilted iron bed. I changed into the school dress that hung behind the door. Then, with some trepidation, I found my way into the main school hall. By that time it was four in the afternoon and, it seemed, hundreds of girls were milling around, talking and giggling, moving outside through the main doors. I waited in the hallway until my godmother came, together with Mother Superior who ushered me into her study.

"We are very happy to have you here," said Mother Superior. "Sister has told me you are hard-working. We would be grateful if you would help the Sisters in the morning, before breakfast, and in the evening after supper. Sometimes we are so busy we hardly have time to pray!"

Since I only prayed in bed, I wondered what she meant. But I readily agreed to help.

"Sister will take you to meet some classmates. Have supper with them, then go along with Sister afterwards."

A group of three girls sat talking on the green outside the school. They stood up as we approached. Sister Alphana introduced me.

"This is Hermione Kohl, my god-daughter," she said. "I know you will be nice to her."

As she bustled away, the girls glanced at one another, then at me. Then the questions came.

"I'm Inga. Where do you come from?"

"Neustift, in the countryside."

"I am from Vienna." Inga pushed her round glasses back on her nose.

She looked very intelligent.

"Hello, my name is Tamara. I'm Russian. Can you speak any languages?"

"No."

"I can speak Russian, French and English..as well as German," she boasted. Her dark eyes, black hair and slender body, made her look like a ballet dancer.

"What's your best subject? I'm Renata, by the way." The third girl was chubbier than the others.

"I don't know."

"I'm best at History." Renata's round face smiled like the moon. "My father is a surgeon in the hospital. What does your father do?"

"My father is....dead."

They fell silent as the bell rang for supper.

The refectory was lined with long, wooden tables, polished enough to reflect your face. A hush descended whilst everyone stood behind the benches to say grace, led by Mother Superior. Then we walked silently up to the servers with our plates and were given a good portion of soup, followed by potatoes, vegetables and meat.

One girl on each table cleared the plates, after which we went up to help ourselves to pudding. I thought the food was delicious, especially as I had not cooked it myself!

"Pigswill," muttered Tamara, as she sat next to me with her dessert.

"It's not bad," I proffered.

"You wait till breakfast!"

After we had eaten, I saw Sister Alphana beckon to me to follow her.

"Your godmother wants you," said Inga. "We`ll meet you in the dormitory later."

"No! I have to ...." I stuttered. "I have my own room."

The girls stared after me in astonishment as I hurried out.

In the kitchen, a hundred or more plates were piled in the sinks. Dirty pots and pans stood on the cooking stove. A tiny nun, wrapped round in a large white apron, her sleeves rolled up, was struggling to lift a cauldron from the fire.

"Thank goodness you`ve come," she said, grumpily. "Hot water is in the kettles." She pointed to several large, black kettles sitting on an open fire.

I was just about to fetch hot water when she shouted "Go away! Take off your school uniform and put working clothes on at once."

I was not sure what `working clothes` were, but I went back to my little room, changed into my skirt and blouse, and returned to the kitchen.

"The apron`s behind the door," said the little nun, arms deep in hot water.

Just then the bell for Compline rang in the distance.

"I never get finished in time," she sighed.

"Let me," I said, taking the dishmop from her hand.

She stayed helping me, showing me where everything was stored away and what to do first thing in the morning.

Over the term, we became quite chatty. I told her all about the farm. She could see I was very accomplished in housework and baking.

"We'll keep this our secret," she agreed.

So from then on, I rose at six to help in the kitchen, changed into my uniform at eight to breakfast with my classmates, spent the day in lessons with them and then disappeared at seven to work as a housemaid until bedtime at nine.

"I have to study," I lied, when they queried where I was off to.

"You must be very rich to have a room to yourself," Tamara said enviously.

When I arrived home for Christmas, the farmhouse seemed very small compared with the huge convent premises. Mother and Wigel were amazed at how I had matured. I caught up on all the news. Joseph came to visit and gave me greetings from the Spritzer family. Josephine and Alois were in our farmhouse with Hedwig and Anna. Franz was already married to a farmer's daughter in the hills and shared his own farm.

It was especially wonderful to see Maria at home once more. She was visiting to introduce us to her fiance from Vienna.

She worked in a city house looking after a Jewish family, who were very kind to her. She told us excitedly that they were going to pay for her wedding reception and give her extra money for her trousseau. We were all to be invited to her wedding. I was thrilled for her, but wished I had a young man.

The only man we schoolgirls came into contact with was the young priest who taught us catechism twice a week, and to whom we made confession. We could not wait to get him alone in the confessional.

"Bless me, Father, for I have sinned." I knelt next to the grill, trying to glimpse his handsome face. It was quite difficult to think of sins.

"I swore in the kitchen, Father, when I dropped a plate."

"Whatever were you doing in the kitchen?" he asked.

"Nothing, Father."

"Well, don't go in there again. That way you will have no cause to swear. Say one Hail Mary, and be a good girl."

"What did he say?" giggled Inga and Tamara when I came out blushing.

" To be a good girl," I answered.

There was not much chance of being otherwise in our situation, but we fell about laughing when we got outside.

As the year passed, my body turned from a child's to a woman's. There was no mirror in my room, but I could see my breasts rounding and my waist thinning. I started my period, but since my sister, Maria, had warned me what to expect, I was prepared. My golden hair grew waist long. I brushed and plaited it, then held it on top of my head pretending to be a fashionable beauty.

(Summer 1935)
Inga, Tamara, Renata and I remained good friends. We spent our days learning together and exchanging views. Renata's father was a doctor in the hospital and often came to visit her, occasionally accompanied by student doctors who were learning under him. Inga came from a wealthy Viennese family who sent her parcels of food which she shared with us. Tamara's family had escaped from Russia during the Revolution and lived in Graz, so she went home each night. They never discovered my secret.

On warm, sunny afternoons we sat in the grounds shared by the convent and the hospital, reading or sewing. As the summer grew hotter, we would fling ourselves down on the grass after lessons and lay with our faces to the sun.

One afternoon, as we were splayed out on the green near the hospital, one of the young student doctors walked over to us.

"Glad to see you enjoying the sun," he said affably. "Sunbathing is very good for you. Only it's better with no clothes on."

We shrieked with laughter.

"You could easily sunbathe on the flat roof, up there." He pointed to the ramparts of our school where the chimneys were flanked by flat walkways.

"It's hot enough. Bye!"

We watched him walk away with amusement. He was not very good-looking and probably thought he was the cat's whiskers. But he did have a point.

"Shall we?" whispered Renata.

"Of course not." Tamara tossed her black curls and jumped up.

"I'm going to get up there," announced Inga. "Last one to follow me is a cissie."

We rushed into the cool, empty dormitory and out on to the back stairs. There we climbed up the flight leading to the attic and pushed open the loft door. The sun slanted down and bounced off the tiled roof, leaving the little walkway half in shade.

"Come on!" urged Inga.

We stood high on the ramparts and peered over. People looked very small in the distance.

"No-one can see us up here," I said.

Renata undid her dress and slipped out of it. We all followed. Then we spread our dresses out and lay down in the sunshine.

"This isn't naked," said Inga. "No-one would know if we were."

"Take all our clothes off!" I exclaimed. "Knickers and everything?"

"I don't think there's anything wrong in being naked," Inga said. "Anyway married people see each other like that, don't they?"

"They do," agreed Renata, knowingly.

"The sun will get to every part of us then," Inga assured us. "Ever so good for our skin."

We carefully stripped, placing our underwear in little piles under our heads. Suddenly, we were in awe of each other's bodies. We saw smooth-skinned, trim, adolescent women.

"We're gorgeous!" said Tamara, stretching full out, her arms held to the sun.

"We're sun babies!" we shouted as we turned over, face down, to dream.

We could hear voices way down in the distance, but no-one would find us here. It was a good hideaway.

We turned over onto our backs. We breathed in deeply, feeling the sun heat our skins, lying with closed eyes against its rays.

How long he had been standing watching us, we never knew. But the   devious student had somehow followed us and was leaning against a chimney stack with his arms folded and his lips grinning.

We never did that again!   And how on earth was I going to admit this in confession?

Mother Superior summoned me into her study the following morning.

"Hermione Kohl," she said, looking at me over her rimmed spectacles, `I have been hearing many things about you."

I nearly fainted on the spot.

"Yes, Mother?"

"That you are a good worker, in class as well as in the kitchens."

"Thank you, Mother."

"So I wish you to attend the interviews for a governess, this afternoon. Make sure you are outside my office at three."

Several other pupils were sitting nervously in the hall waiting to be called into the office.
When it was my turn, I smoothed down my school uniform and stepped in.   Three smartly

dressed women sat beside the desk waiting to look me over.

Mother Superior introduced me.

"What subjects do you excel in?" asked one lady, who wore a perky straw hat with a black net veil.

"I..er," I stuttered.

"She is at the top of her class," interceded Mother Superior.

"Can you cook ?" asked a very large woman.

"Very well," I replied with honesty. "I can make bread and cakes."

"A good farm-hand too, I believe. We have farms outside Graz. Do you care to work on a farm?" she continued.

I nodded, but thought that was the last thing I wanted.

"I have four children," offered a very glamorous lady in a flowing dress. "Some of them belong to my husband, Professor List, and some are mine. Are you good with children?"

"I think so. I helped with my own sisters."

"Mine - ours - are three boys and a little girl." She spoke quietly and seemed very kind. I prayed to be chosen by her.

"Thank you, Hermione." Mother Superior dismissed me with a wave of her hand.

My three friends were waiting for me anxiously. We were all in a nervous state because our exams were not far away and we knew our futures depended on the results.

"What happened?" They crowded round.

"Nothing. They just looked me over," I replied.

"I suppose I shall end up as a governess," said Tamara, whose family had fallen on hard times.

"I'm going to be a nurse," Renata assured us. "I'll probably study here, in Daddy's hospital."

Inga waltzed around singing `Some day my Prince will come!`

"Well, I want to be a Governess," I said. " So long as I can work for Frau List. She is so elegant and romantic."

I was full of thoughts of romance. When Mother Superior announced that all three ladies wanted me, I insisted that I wanted to work only for Frau and Professor List. They were a high-class family, and I intended to go up in the world.

My happy, hard-working school days ended with the four of us vowing to love each other for ever and never to forget each other.

"Give me your address, Hermione," said Inga. "So that we can write to each other."

"Well, at present my family live in Vienna," I lied, giving her the address where my sister,

Maria, was housekeeper. We all exchanged addresses and promised to keep in touch.

By August I was back in Neustift, helping with the harvest, waiting for a letter from Frau and Professor List. When it arrived I was bitterly disappointed. They had found an interim governess, who would stay with them for a year, after which they would be happy to employ me.

I had loved my time in Graz and found it difficult to settle back into farm life.

"I have decided to return to Graz," I informed Mother and Wigel one morning. "I`ve asked my godmother to find me a position."

Mother looked disappointed.

"Are you certain that is what you want?" she asked. "There`s a nice young farmer near here who is interested in you."

I snorted. "The last thing I want to be is a farmer`s wife!"

Wigel put his arm around Mother and smiled.

"It`s not so bad," he said, giving her a squeeze.

A few weeks later, I packed my few belongings, hugged Mother and my younger sisters `Goodbye`, and set off for a hotel in Graz. I was to learn to be an apprentice cook, working in the kitchens for six months. It was hard work, but I learned to make sauces and exotic soups. I learned to serve wiener-schnitzels with side vegetables. I learned to make delicious desserts.

I enjoyed preparing and presenting the food, but at the end of my time there I felt that, even though I was well qualified to be a cook, I would rather be a governess. I was just eighteen, full of energy and verve. I did not want to slave over a hot stove, thank you very much. I wanted to look after the List children, with all the amenities of a rich household. It would not be total freedom, but it would give me a kind of independence to work in my own way. So I waited.

In the meantime, my older sister, Maria, was courting her army officer in Vienna and was about to be married. Perhaps I would meet someone of my own at her wedding.

7 MARIA

(Summer 1937)

The sun shone warmly on Maria's wedding day.
Everyone in my family was gathering together
for the celebration.   Her big day was to be in
Hapsburg, about eighteen kilometres from our
farm. Hedwig, Anna and I put on our best floral
dresses and set off early to walk there. Alois
accompanied us as escort, leaving Mother and
Wigel to follow on later in the cart. Josephine
joined us as we passed the farm where she
worked.

Many neighbours from our village had been
invited to the two o'clock wedding. We made a
merry procession on our way across the valleys.
We were all sturdy hikers, well used to traversing
our beautiful mountains,   eager to arrive on time
for the festivities in Hapsburg.

Franz Hagenhoffer, whose family owned a
flourishing coffee shop in Hapsburg, was the
bridegroom. He was ten years older than Maria
and a serving officer in the Austrian Army,

"Do you love him?" I asked Maria, when she
had confided that she was to be married.

"I think so," she said. "He's tall and very good-
looking, but you never really know 'till you live
with someone, do you?"

I agreed. Anyway, I was not at all sure whether marrying a man that old was such a good idea.

Organ music flooded the church as my tall, shapely sister, in her white wedding dress, walked down the aisle on Wigel`s arm. At the altar, her distinguished-looking bridegroom stood waiting nervously. As Maria reached him, they clasped each other`s hands. My heart lifted. I knew they were right for each other.

Maria`s employer, Dr. Schnabel from Vienna, had insisted on contributing to the expense. He, with his wife and children, stayed at the nearby hotel, where a huge wedding breakfast had been organised.

As we left the church we could hear the strains of the Blue Danube waltz bouncing down the road, welcoming us to the party. Jovial guests kissed one another as they met each other, pleased to see each other again and eager to join in the festivities.

An Austrian band struck up as we entered the room. Beaming musicians, dressed in plus fours, white shirts, green ties and coloured braces, pumped their accordions rhythmically, so that we could not help tapping our feet in time with the music as we sat down for the meal.

No expense was spared. There were two kinds of soup, followed by roast beef and pork, potatoes, vegetables and salads. Set out along the tables was a great variety of delicious cakes, all to be eaten. Red and white wine filled our glasses. By the time we were expected to dance, we could hardly move. But dance we did, waltzing and jigging, even prancing to the polka.

Every one of my brothers danced with me, but Joseph most of all. Then Wigel, then the bridegroom himself.

"Your turn next, little sister," he said, twirling me round the dance floor.

Hedwig and I laughingly flopped into chairs by the side just as a toast was raised to the happy couple. Several guests had brought along their own special wedding cakes as gifts. We cheered as Maria and Franz cut one, then another, then the next. We had never had such dancing, such food and drink, such fun!

Later in the evening, wedding cake and doughnuts were served with more coffee and liqueurs.

"I'm feeling quite tipsy," I admitted to Josephine, who looked rather bleary-eyed as well.

"I feel like a little drink," she giggled, as she went to the bar.

She came back with two small glasses filled with yellow custard.

"Go on, taste it," she prompted.

"Yuk, what is it?"

"Advocaat...dip your finger in and suck. It's delicious."

It was! We managed one more little glass each, by which time it was dark outside and time to walk home.

"I do hope you will be happy, Maria darling," I said, as I kissed her goodbye.

"I'll enjoy working in the family coffee shop," she said, smiling joyfully. "And I do love my husband."

The whole village seemed to be with us as we walked back to our homes in the dark. Moonlight paled our faces. The cool air encouraged us to keep up the pace. Night owls watched alertly as the merry throng passed by. I arrived home weary but elated; my heavy limbs aching, my head beginning to hurt as I flung myself on to my bed. It was the best wedding I had ever been to. I drifted off to sleep imagining my own.

A letter from Frau List arrived the following week. It told me to report to their home in Graz at the beginning of September. A new life was about to start for me as well.

8   THE LIST FAMILY

(March 1938, Anschluss, German invasion of Austria.)

The large property of Professor Dr. Hans List was surrounded by a high, red brick wall into which wrought iron gates were set. I pushed these open and walked along the gravel driveway feeling very apprehensive. Sweeping steps led up to the huge front door. I clutched the small suitcase containing my meagre belongings, rang the bell and waited. A tall, well-dressed lady eventually stood on the threshold.

"Yes?"

She looked older than Frau List as I had remembered her, but I blurted out, "Gnadige Frau List, I am Hermione Kohl."

"I am not the lady of the house," she laughed. "Come in, please. I am the housekeeper, Tilda."

She beckoned me into the vestibule, then on through inner glass doors which opened onto a marble hall. It was grander than I had ever imagined.

"Please follow me."

I was led up the grand staircase, where oil paintings of ancestors stared down sternly, making me feel very small.

The housekeeper knocked gently on one of the many doors. A voice inside sang, "Come in."

Frau List rose from the chaise-longue and extended her hand.

"Thank you, Tilda." She dismissed her housekeeper. "Do sit down, Hermione," she said, kindly.

She was truly beautiful with a tall, slender figure and sparkling eyes. The room appeared to be her personal sitting-room. A large grand piano, with its top open, stood near the balcony window overlooking sweeping lawns. Fine carpets and furniture gave the room a warm, lived-in feeling. I perched myself on the edge of a chair.

"Now, tell me all about yourself."

By the time I had recounted my life story, I felt wonderfully at ease.

"I think you will fit in very well," she said. "Let me explain about my family. My husband is Austrian and has two sons by his first wife. Harold, the eldest, lives with us. Manfred lives with his mother but stays here sometimes. I am German, as is my boy, Osrid," she added, proudly. "Our little girl, Dagmar, is the result of Austrian-German unity - like our countries." She laughed. "Now let me show you around my home."

A tour of the house revealed that the kitchen, reception rooms, library and Prof. List`s study were all on the ground floor, as were his mother`s apartments. Frau List`s rooms were on the first floor, next to the large dining-room, beside which was a smaller kitchen for heating plates and dishes.

"This can be used by you to make emergency meals for the nursery," she said.

She turned to open another door. I gasped as I entered. Turquoise silk drapes framed large windows; ebony furniture held silk embroidered cushions. An ornately carved mirror hung over the fireplace. She stepped proudly into the centre of a delicately coloured carpet.

"This is our Chinese sitting-room. Do you like it?"

"It's wonderful!" I breathed.

"The wall hanging was a gift to my husband from the Chinese Embassy. It's a room we use infrequently," she added. "Never with the children."

I nodded.

On the next floor were more living quarters, bathrooms and children's bedrooms.

"There you are, Mary," said my Lady, as she entered the nursery.

My predecessor was squatting on the floor, helping a toddler to build a brick tower. She jumped up as we appeared.

"Mary is leaving at the end of this week to get married. I am sure she will show you the ropes before she goes."

Mary and I grinned at each other.

"This is our little girl, Dagmar," Frau List smiled at her baby, but made no attempt to pick her up.

"Osrid is probably with Anna, our cook, tasting something or other," she continued. "He`s nearly five, so he is going to school next term. Just in time." She gave Mary a knowing glance.

Finally, the door onto a large sun-filled bedroom was opened. Two huge wardrobes stood against one wall. There was a large double bed flanked by neat side-cupboards and comfortable chairs. An antique desk, with writing paper laid on top, stood by the window overlooking the back garden.

"This is your room now," said Frau List. "Please make yourself at home. I will see you at supper time."

I sat quietly on the edge of the bed collecting my thoughts. This was about as far away as one could get from the farmhouse. There was a homely elegance everywhere. I was enchanted by it.

I hung my coat and Sunday-best dress in a cupboard. There were two white dresses inside which I supposed were my nurse`s outfits. I splashed my face in the wash basin and looked in the mirror. A rather pretty young lady, with golden hair tied in a bun, stared back.

Suddenly, the door burst open. Two school-boys stood in the doorway, grinning madly.

"Hello. I'm Harold. I'm the eldest. I'm twelve. This is Manfred, my brother, He's staying here for now," said one.

"Hello!" I held out my hand, which they shook vigorously, clicking their heels.

"Your mother showed me your rooms," I began, realising my mistake.

"She's not our mother," interrupted Manfred. "We're not German."

"Our family are a bit of both really," said Harold affably. "Papa was married before. He's Austrian. Mutter (Frau List) and Osrid are German."

"But Dagmar is only half of each," finished Manfred.

"See you at supper!" cried Manfred as they pushed past each other into the nursery, where I could hear them greeting Mary and baby Dagmar.

I followed after them. A sturdy dark-haired boy had appeared.

"Are you Osrid?" I asked.

He nodded. "What's your name?"

"Hermione - but you can call me Mina. All right?"

By suppertime, we were the best of friends. On the dot of seven, a gong sounded below.

"Wash your hands and face," Mary told the boys, as she cleaned Dagmar's face before carrying her downstairs.

Osrid led me by the hand into the dining-room. Professor Dr. List and his wife were already seated at each end of the large dining-table.

"Good evening, Mutter, Papa," said the boys in unison, as they took their places and waited to be served.

Dagmar was lifted into her high-chair between Mary and Osrid. I stood apart, unsure of where to sit, since there were two spare places laid.

Professor Dr. List stood up and held a chair for me, saying "We hope you will be very happy here."

As I murmured, "Thank you, sir," the door was flung open and an elderly lady, with a walking stick, strode in to take her place.

"Good-evening, everybody," she intoned, unfolding her napkin.

She did not seem to notice me. She tapped her stick on the ground twice, which seemed to be the signal for the meal to commence. We were waited upon by the housekeeper, Tilda, and a young maid who winked at me. Everyone ate in silence, except when the Professor asked the boys questions and they answered politely. My farmhouse meals were truly miles away.

After supper, I was taken downstairs to meet Anna, the cook. All of a sudden,I was surrounded by jumping poodles trying to lick my face.

"Animals!" I exclaimed happily.

"They're a proper nuisance, always getting under my feet," said Anna crisply. "I prefer cats myself. They know how to look after themselves."

"The strudel was delicious," I told her.

She beamed at me.

"I'll show you how to make it. You ask me, old Annie, whenever you want the recipe," she replied.

"Hello, I'm Josie," said the young housemaid who had winked at me. "I'll show you around Graz on our day off."

"I know Graz," I said. "I went to school here."

"Then you know the park with the boating lake?"

"No."

"I'll show you Saturday afternoon if you like."

Josie and I walked out of the gates together that weekend.

"There's something I must do first," I said, pushing my letter home into the post-box. "I want to buy a book to write recipes in."

"You don't have to do any cooking!" exclaimed Josie.

"I know. I want to write down Annie's recipes."

"Whatever for?"

"My future," I said, confidently.

The park was crowded with family outings. Josie led me down to the lakeside where boats could be hired out to rowers.

"Let's take one." I had never been in a boat before, but I was keen to try.

"I can't row," Josie said.

"I can," I lied.

The boat slid away from the edge. I took the oars and began to row. Soon we were skimming over the water.

"You're good. You must have had lots of practice," said Josie, reclining like a lady. "Let's bring the children next time."

When Mary left, the children became my sole charge. The boys were well-behaved and polite, keen to study and find out everything. Baby Dagmar took to me immediately, planting kisses on my face as I cuddled her.

"I do love looking after babies," I thought.

Which was just as well, since I soon learned that another little List was on the way.

9 RESPONSIBILITIES

(September 1938)

The daily routine started at six-thirty. During school term the boys and Professor Dr List breakfasted early and had left by seven forty-five. When Osrid started school, I walked him there with Dagmar in her pram.

Annie saw to the meals, while Tilda, the housekeeper, looked after the house, helped by Josie. There was also a gardener, Karl, to work outside. All I had to do was play with Dagmar in the garden and walk the poodles.

Very soon, neighbours would call for Frau List and leave their children with me. It was like running a children's home, especially during school holidays. We played hide-and-seek behind the bushes and fir trees, and catch-me-if-you-can, running around the vegetable patches much to Karl's annoyance.

"Hey! Keep off my garden," he yelled, as we skirted round rows of cauliflowers and Brussels sprouts, leeks and lettuces. Soft fruit bushes and strawberry beds spread towards bean poles and tomato cloches, beyond which was the chicken coop. We screamed happily as we played tag around them.

We used skipping ropes to make high-jumps; bowled hoops along the driveway; whipped tops into dizzy spinning whirls. We crouched on the ground, counted out coloured marbles and tried to knock the black one.

"I won!" cried Osrid, who had not.

Boys rolled on the grass in a good-natured free-for-all, then bounced on to me for piggyback rides.

Every evening, with the children gathered in the nursery, I told them fairy stories. By ten o'clock I was in bed, exhausted.

It was the rule that the boys made their own beds, tidied their rooms and cleaned their shoes.

"One day you will have servants to look after you," said the Professor at lunch-time. "So you had better learn now the right way to do things."

"But..," whispered Osrid.

"No `buts`," ordered his step-father.

"I can't reach over my bed yet."

"I'll help you," I said quietly.

"Not too much," warned the Professor.

Frau List appeared in a silk dressing-gown.

"I feel frail today," she sighed. "Mina, will you see to our week's groceries? I have some sort of list. Check with cook and Tilda. Oh, and darling," to her husband, "Please give Mina the money."

Both Annie and Tilda looked askance when I reported my new task, but they complied. We all had special purchases for our jobs and the order was enormous. It was going to be very costly.

I was quite nervous on my way to the shops. I had never held so much money so it was carefully tucked out of sight in Dagmar's pram.

The shopkeeper ticked each item on the list: coffee, butter, milk, sugar, flour, raisins, herrings, veal, pork sausage-worsht, floor-polish, starch, soap and a scrubbing brush.

"Delivery this evening, Fraulein? Tell them it will be thirty-five schillings."

To his surprise, I paid on the spot. From then on I organised the weekly shopping.

On my next afternoon off, I visited my godmother at her convent.

"My, you look well, Mina!" She welcomed me with a kiss.

"The List children are so nice. I couldn't be happier.

Sister Alphana laughed. "You will enjoy your own children, one day."

She clasped her hands together and looked up. "Let us pray that peace lasts, my dear. Heaven knows what is happening in Germany."

(Christmas 1938)
On Sundays I walked with the family to the catholic church. The tall priest, Father Martin with his black beard, terrified me. He seemed

stern and forbidding. Just before Christmas was the time to make my confession. I hesitated before stepping into the Confessional.

"Bless me, Father, for I have sinned," I whispered.

"I doubt that, my child."

My mouth dropped open.

"Go on, my child."

"I am happy here, but sometimes I yearn to go home."

"That`s only natural."

"Sometimes I wish I had time for myself. My lady never gets up for breakfast, she rests every afternoon. She never does a stroke of work. I am guilty of envy, Father."

"I expect `my lady` envies you your youth and vitality," he chuckled. "Say three `Hail Mary`s` and God bless you."

On Christmas Eve, the house was festive with greenery and decorations. A huge tree stood in the hallway covered with tinsel and candles. The staff entered Frau List`s sitting room to receive gifts, handed solemnly to us by the children.

"May I take the boys to midnight mass?" I asked.

"It will be a great excitement," agreed their mother.

The church was crowded. We jostled to the manger where the boys lit candles.

We sang `O Tannenbaum` and `Stille Nacht` with the choir. The service was taken by a priest I did not recognise. He had the stature of Father Martin, the same voice. It took me a while to realise it was Father Martin with his black beard shaved off.

(Spring 1939)

Baby Gertrude was born safely. Her little cot was placed in my room and she was immediately my responsibility. During the night I used the cooker in the little kitchen to heat her bottle. Bleary-eyed, I sat on my bed to feed her, listening to her suck like the baby lambs I had reared.

My lady rested all day and went out in the evenings. By the time it was Whitsun, I realised I had not had one day off for months.

"May I take time off, to see my family?" I asked her.

Frau List pulled a face.

"Just for a few days," I persisted.

"It is a little awkward. I have a great many concerts and parties to attend. However.." she sighed, "For a day or two. You may go Wednesday."

She looked very put out.

"I suppose you will have to place Gertrude's cot in my room tomorrow," she said.

That night Osrid crept into my bed in the early hours. He seemed hot and feverish. Dagmar was restless and grizzly. How could I leave them? By the end of the week they had developed chickenpox. Manfred, who was visiting for the holidays, went down with it as well.

"I hope you do not catch it, Mina," worried Frau List.

"I'm too busy to be ill," I said.

Baby Gertrude had a small blister on her arm, but the disease did not develop in her. Harold, who had had chickenpox and was immune, helped me dab calamine lotion on his brothers and sister. Annie made enough warm blackcurrant and lemon drinks to keep us going.

"Tell us a story," pleaded Osrid, tucked up with the others in the nursery.

"All right, but this one is a big secret. You won't tell, will you?"

They solemnly shook their heads.

"You know the planes that drone around the sky. Well, one of them is flown by my pilot."

"*Your* pilot?"

"When he sees me in the garden he dips his wings at me. Haven't you noticed?"

"I have," said Osrid.

"How do you know it is your pilot?" asked Harold.

"He threw me down a note - that he loves me - this very morning."

"I heard the plane!" exclaimed Osrid.

"Show us your note then," said Manfred.

"I couldn`t do that." I put my finger to my lips. "I told you it`s a big secret. If his officer found out, he would be for the high jump."

"Parachute out?" said Osrid.

"I would never be able to see him again."

"But *we `ve* never seen him," pouted Osrid.

"Is it true? Really true?" asked Manfred.

I nodded and we all giggled.

Professor Dr. List sent for me in his study next afternoon. I could not think what I had done.

"Sit down, Mina." He leaned back in his chair and clasped his hands together. "I understand you have a boyfriend."

"I...no!" I stammered.

"Well, I have it on good authority that a certain air pilot loves you."

"My goodness!" I cried, my face hot with blushing.

He looked at me over his glasses and smiled.

"There`s nothing to be ashamed of, is there?"

"It`s a story! I just told a story to keep them amused."

"Ahh..so it is untrue?"

"Well..yes." I wished I had never thought up such a tale.

"It might well be true, soon enough."

Professor List took off his glasses and wiped them. "There is a garrison of Germans to be stationed outside Graz. A great deal of trouble is brewing, my dear."

By the beginning of August there were more planes in the sky than ever. German soldiers walked about the town in groups.

"There's going to be war," said Annie soberly, as we sat talking in the kitchen. "I can't bear the thought."

"My father was killed in the last war, at Ypres." said Tilda. "Life is never the same, ever."

Josie moved restlessly around the room, twisting her handkerchief into knots.

"I have three brothers," she said.

I started to understand.

"So have I," I murmured.

PART TWO

*The War
(1939 - 1945)*

10 WAR

*(September 1939 Germany invades Poland.
War declared on Germany)*

"We are all going on an outing today," announced the Professor at weekend breakfast.

"Annie has organised a picnic," Frau List told me. "Get the children ready to go to our farm."

"Harvest time!" screamed Osrid. "Can I go on the tram with Mina? Can I?"

We were ready to set off in an hour. Professor List drove his car from the garage and opened the door for his wife to sit in front. Annie, baby Gertrude and Grandmother, sat grandly in the back. We waved them through the gate, shouting, "See you there!"

Harold, Osrid and Dagmar skipped round me to the tram-stop. Tilda, Josie and Karl, the gardener, with his boy, stepped on behind us. The tram rattled through the centre of Graz to the outskirts, then out to Egendorf, where we dismounted and walked the mile to the family farm.

Summer had been good and crops were ripe and plentiful. Karl and his boy, with the Professor helping, set about digging up vegetables. Potatoes, onions, carrots, turnips, parsnips were lifted, soil shaken off, then packed into canvas sacks.

Osrid and Josie, with Dagmar trying to help, held the ladders as Harold and I climbed into apple trees to fill our bags with eaters and cookers. Frau List picked peaches and cherries, alongside Annie and Tilda, while Grandmother dangled Gertrude on her lap.

Later, everyone helped to stow baskets of fruit into the car-boot, to be taken home for preserving. The heavy main crops were to be brought along by truck. By the end of the harvest we were exhausted, but elated.

Annie worked hard to stock the larder up with jars of jam, preserved peaches, cherries and sauerkraut.

By the end of the weekend, sacks of potatoes and onions were stored in the cellar, alongside other root vegetables and stocks of fuel. Large bags of rice, flour and sugar had been bought in. Blocks of salt and pickles stood on shelves.

"This should see us out till the war ends," said cook confidently.

(Spring 1940)
On my way to the shops, I watched planes leaving white tails in the clear, cold sky.

"Coffee beans, please." I studied the shopping list.

"We're out," said the shopkeeper sullenly. "What's more, next week it's on ration, along with everything else."

"We need the usual butter order, cornflour, vinegar, raisins…"

"Hold on!" Several other commodities were out of stock.

"That will be fifty schillings," he said, totting up the bill.

"What? That's twice as much as last week!"

"Right. It will be twice as much next week," he replied. "And you can blame that on the bloody war!"

As I walked back, armoured cars and troop lorries jammed the street. Soldiers leant over the sides and whistled as I turned into our street.

Frau List called for me next morning.

"We are expecting an important visitor this afternoon. Please make sure the children are neat and tidy when they return from school. Wait for me to call you down with them."

Osrid arrived home just before Harold. Manfred was with him, since he was on one of his visits. They excitedly changed into their best suits and brushed their hair. I dressed Dagmar in her prettiest clothes, tied a ribbon on top of baby Gertrude's hair, and put on my clean nurse's dress.

We rushed to look out of Harold`s front window as a large black limousine slid into the driveway. A uniformed officer jumped out to open the rear passenger door. We watched silently as Doctor Goebbels (Reichs-Minister of Propaganda) mounted the steps to our front door.

Eventually, Josie, in her posh maid`s outfit, came to summon us. We were shown into the Chinese room where Frau List sat elegantly on the settee.

Doctor Goebbels sat beside her, smiling thinly. Professor List stood by the fireplace looking stern. Frau List beckoned us into the centre of the room.

"These are my husband`s boys, Harold and Manfred," she said. The two boys stood to attention and bowed.

"This is my son, Osrid."

Osrid stood awkwardly, staring. His mother murmured "Go on!" and he suddenly clicked his heels, shouted "Heil Hitler!" and made the Nazi salute. The older boys copied him immediately.

Goebbels offered his hand, which they solemnly shook in turn.

"Here is my lovely, little Dagmar," said my lady. "And baby Gertrude with Hermione."

The hand was extended to me as Dagmar clung tightly to my skirt.

"How do you do?" I muttered as he took my hand limply.

"My family is just like yours," said Doctor Goebbels. "Five beautiful children. It is them we are fighting for."

Frau List beamed. Professor Dr. List turned away slightly. The expression on his face, reflected in the mirror, was one of disgust.

"Thank you, Mina," he said, as he turned towards me. "Take the children to the nursery now, and please tell them one of your stories."

But I did not feel like telling happy tales. Letters from home told me that first Alois, now Joseph, had been called up into the army. That night I read `Cinderella` to the children just to cheer myself up.

Frau Elfrieda List called me into her sitting room after lunch the following day.

"The Professor has been sent to Heidelberg on an important mission," she said. "Grandmother is a little upset. Please go down to comfort her."

(June 1940)
The Professor returned looking tired and thin. He seemed preoccupied, spending all his time in the study and eating meals there. His wife curtailed most of her social life and spent more evenings at home, playing the piano to selected guests, several of whom were German officers.

One afternoon, another important visitor sat in the Chinese room. The boys were at school, but I was called down to show off Dagmar and Gertrude.

A heavily built, affable-looking officer sat relaxed and smiling.

"Here is the Reichs-Field-Marshal responsible for your pilot," said Professor List, jokingly.

I blushed.

"Pilots in the Luftwaffe are the best in the world," said Hermann Goering, jovially. "All the girls love my pilots."

Frau List rose to stand by the window as the engines of Heinkel bombers pulsed overhead.

"Destination England," said the Field-Marshal. "We will have peace by the end of this year."

11 JOSEF

(Summer 1941)

In July, an irate Frau List announced that another baby was on the way.

"I feel extremely unwell," she sighed over Saturday lunch. "You can't possibly have time off this weekend, Mina. I couldn't possibly manage baby Gertrude and Dagmar for even an afternoon." She held the back of her hand to her forehead as she left the table to lie down.

Grandmother tutted, "It's a good thing I'm around to help." She turned to me. "Off you go. Leave the girls with me for a couple of hours."

"I'll take the boys to the lake," I said. "Josie and I promised them a boating trip."

Josie handed me the oars as I climbed aboard after the boys.

"I can row, can't I?" said Osrid, bouncing in the stern.

"No, you can't," said Harold. "I can. Move over, Mina."

I shrieked as he stood up and tried to grab an oar from me. One oar fell into the water with a splash, and the boat floated away from the side, wobbling precariously.

Josie stood on the bank laughing uncontrollably.

"Oh, honestly!" I tried to manoeuvre back with one oar.

"Can we help?" shouted two soldiers, running down the bank.

"I can manage, thank you!" I called, leaning out to try to pick up the floating oar.

"We're sinking!" cried the boys.

I pulled myself back in. Sure enough, water was lapping at my shoes.

"The boat's letting in water!" I yelled.

One of the soldiers waded in, grabbed the hull and pulled us to safety.

"Caught you!" he said.

His friend lifted out Osrid, then helped Harold over to Josie. My rescuer smiled, put his hands round my waist and jumped me onto the bank.

"Thank you!" I gasped, looking up at the brightest blue eyes I had ever seen. My heart leapt as I thought, *"This man is mine!"*

"Can I walk you home?" he said later, stepping along by my side after we had said `goodbye`. "What's your name?"

"Hermione. Yours?"

"Josef."

"My favourite name," I said.

"That's good," he laughed.

Osrid hugged me as I tucked him in bed that night.

"Your eyes are misty," he whispered. "I liked that soldier."

"So did I," I replied.

"Mina's met her pilot. Only he's a soldier," announced Osrid, with confidence, next day at lunch.

"Really?" Frau List perked up.

"No, of course not," I said.

But I made an excuse to take Gertrude and Dagmar for a walk. My heart leapt as I saw him standing by the wall, hidden from the iron gates.

"How did you know?" I asked.

"I knew."

We walked silently to the park, just glad to be together. Dagmar and Gertrude toddled on the grass as we sat down to talk. Of everything. Our homes, our lives, our hopes, our thoughts.

"It is wonderful, having someone to talk to," Josef confided.

"Don't you have friends in the army?"

"It's not the same. Everyone is thrown together, jumbled up. None of us want to be there. We are treated like things, not people. I hate being ordered about."

"I'm ordered about," I said.

"You're not ordered to kill, are you?"

"No."

He squeezed my hand.

"It will soon be over, I'm sure," I said.

"I hope so, but I don`t think it. We are awaiting our posting."

"You`re leaving!" I cried.

"Not yet. Don`t get upset.We`ll meet somehow." He put his arm around my shoulder. "Look at the children," he laughed.

Dagmar, with Gertrude toddling after, was intent on trying to catch a butterfly. I sighed and gathered the girls into their pram. We were both so tied up that being together would take a miracle.

"I`ll walk back to the house with you," Josef said.

He held the iron gates open for the pram.

"Come in with me," I pleaded.

Several faces were pressed against the windows as we went round to the back garden. Josie came running out of the kitchen.

"I`ll take the children," she beamed at us. "My lady says you can have half an hour together before supper."

We ran, hand in hand, out of the driveway, like children escaping from school. After that, every time I left the house I searched for him. Sometimes he was waiting by the wall. Sometimes we spotted each other across the park, or in the street by the church and raced to be together.

Often he was not there, but letters appeared in the letter-box, addressed to me.

"Frau List wants to see you," said Josie. "In her bedroom."

My lady was sitting up in bed, looking better.

"You have found your man," she said. "It is so romantic."

I blushed.

"Look, there's an abundance of fruit needing to be picked," she went on. "Perhaps you would do that for me?"

I stood open-mouthed. Surely she did not expect me to do the gardener's job!

"But.." I muttered, seeing all my precious spare moments snatched away.

She laughed at my look.

"At Egendorf," she explained. "Alone."

Josef and I sat in the tram, closely pressed together. It was a lovely, long journey and we arrived at the farm more than contented to be together.

"Well, I just have to pick cherries," I said laughingly. "Otherwise, goodness knows what my lady will think."

"Right then." He propped up the ladder. "Hand me the basket."

Ripe-red cherries tumbled into containers, filling them to the brim.

"Mina?"

"Yes, Josef."

He jumped down and stood, a head taller than me, with both arms round my waist.

"I love you very much."

"Josef!"

"You know that, don`t you?"

I nodded, tears coursing down my cheeks.

"But we can never be together," I sobbed.

"We will always be together." He took out a handkerchief and wiped my eyes. "We belong to each other."

We kissed tenderly, wanting the day to last forever throughout our lives.

"I`ll write twice a week. You do the same. I`ll give you my forwarding address tomorrow."

"Tomorrow!"

"I am being posted. We leave for Russia the day after."

I could not stop crying.

"He`s leaving." I sobbed in the kitchen.

Annie and Josie were sniffling over soup vegetables on the table.

Tilda came down and told me to see Frau List. I did not want to see anybody. I just wanted Josef. Grandmother and Frau List were in the sitting room.

"Mina, dear. I heard your young man is leaving for the front."

I burst into tears again. Grandmother stood up and put her arm around me as I sobbed on her shoulder. "You are seeing him before he goes?"

I managed to nod. "He said he was coming this afternoon."

Frau List rose heavily from her chair, picking up a pair of scissors. "Come into the garden," she said. Grandmother followed. Outside, she cut blooms of bright dahlias, sweet-smelling stocks and colourful roses. My arms were filled with flowers.

"Every year these die, every year they grow anew. You must have faith, my dear."

"You have to help him by being strong," said Grandmother. "I know. I know."

By the time Josef arrived at the house I was quite calm. Tea had been laid for us in the small kitchen. The children were nowhere to be seen. We said our goodbyes quietly and lovingly.

At the iron gate, I handed over my bouquet of flowers. "These are for you, my dearest."

"I can`t take them all," he said, selecting one red rose. "I`ll press this, in my pocket, against my heart."

The warmth of his kiss flooded through me as he pulled away from my arms and disappeared round the corner.

12 AIR RAID

(Spring 1942)

Baby Helmut was born earlier than expected. He was a fractious little boy who kept me awake through the night. With my duties doubled, I was so busy I hardly noticed night from day. Frau List recovered sufficiently to resume her social life, despite the increasing air raid warnings.

The staff sat drinking coffee round the kitchen table, discussing the worsening situation.

"It's only practice," said Annie, as the air raid sirens wailed, followed by the all-clear.

"It's more than that," said Tilda. "Our Professor has been pressured to do war work. He is going to live in Dresden."

"What about her Ladyship?" asked Josie.

"She's staying."

"What about us?" I said.

"We're staying."

Three weeks later, two letters arrived for me. One from my Josef saying he had not heard from me. Did I still love him? I had written to him every spare moment, and posted at least six letters. I wondered why he had not received them.

The other letter was from Mother to say both Alois on our farm, and Joseph on the Spritzer's farm, had been called up along with many other boys from the neighbourhood. She and Wigel were doing their best to keep things going, with help from Hedwig and Anna, and I was to look after myself.

By the next post, call-up papers came for Karl`s son and for Josie to return to her home town to work in a factory. She was horrified.

"It will be a new experience," said Tilda

"The war will soon be over," encouraged Annie, handing Josie a hanky

We knew in our hearts this was untrue. Josie packed and left next day. Tilda and Annie cried for her, but I was dry-eyed. It was certain to be my turn next.

I stood with the children on the steps of the house, as Frau List embraced her husband and kissed him goodbye.` An imposing black limousine, driven by a soldier, waited for him in the driveway. Grandmother leant heavily on her stick, wiping her eyes with a lace handkerchief. Her sister was staying with her these days, and the two elderly ladies helped each other inside with bowed heads.

By the beginning of the next week, real air raids were taking place at night somewhere in the distance. Anti-aircraft bombardments boomed and cracked into the black, starry air. We watched from our bedroom windows as trailer lights flew across the sky, sounds drifting our way long after the flashes.

"It's like a thunderstorm," said Osrid, holding my hand.

"So long as it does not get any nearer," I thought.

Frau List informed us she was going out Friday night and that we were not to worry about her. If need be, she would shelter in the Schlossberg bunker in town.

The sirens went just after midnight. Almost immediately an enormous blast shook all the windows.

"Quick children!" I grabbed baby Helmut, who was sound asleep. I pulled at Gertrude and Dagmar, who sleepily fell out of their beds.

Another ear-splitting bang!

Both Osrid and Harold were up, shouting with fear.

"Go down into the cellar!" I yelled. "Grab blankets, anything."

Harold raced ahead, threw open the cellar door and pulled the light switch as we all skidded downstairs and into the underground storeroom. There were no windows down here to splinter and kill. Sacks of potatoes, humped high, would act as a buffer against explosions. The children slid onto the cold floor, shivering.

"Stand on a blanket. Hold baby!" I plonked Helmut into Harold's arms. "I'm going for Grandmother."

There was another, muffled, continuous explosive sound which rose and died away, after which we heard the tap of Grandmother's stick on the marble floor upstairs. I opened the cellar door. She and Aunt stood there dressed in warm clothes, coats and boots, as if they were going on an outing.

"Be prepared for anything," puffed Grandmother, as she descended the steps and sank on to an old wicker sofa beside her sister. Harold handed back Helmut, who slept soundly on my lap, as the children and I huddled together on the blanket.

The bombardment grew in volume above us. The light bulb dimmed, grew bright, then went out completely, leaving us pressed down by blackness. The children screamed.

"What we need is a candle," said Grandmother in the dark. "I have just the thing."

We could hear her handbag snap open. A match fizzed up like a sparkler and the candle wick began to catch. A soft glow of light illumined the gaunt, frightened faces of the children.

"Grandmother, you are wonderful!" said Harold.

"I've been through this before," she said.

We stayed in the cellar all night, drifting in and out of sleep, until Helmut decided it was time for his feed. His yelling masked the sound of the all-clear that Osrid insisted he could hear away in the distance.

The boys agreed it was safe to go up, so we adults followed. Grandmother opened the front door, where several large pieces of shrapnel lay on the pathway. We stepped round them and went to look outside the iron gates.

A group of onlookers stood in the road. Firemen were calling to each other beside a fire-engine that was pumping water onto a burning bush. Several trees along the road were smouldering. The house two doors away had been completely demolished.

"That`s it!" Frau List announced when she returned, safe and sound. "You are taking my children and Grandmother to the mountains."

"Alone?"

"You can survive in the mountains, can`t you?" she said scornfully.

"Of course I can," I replied. "They are my home."

"I have booked you all into one of our favourite skiing hotels," she added. "I hope it will suit you!"

13 DACHSTEIN

(Summer 1942)
Osrid and Harold filled their haversacks with belongings.   Gertrude and Dagmar had little satchels on their backs.   Grandmother carried a small suitcase and her handbag. I held the baby, with another haversack on my back and a large suitcase filled with provisions.

We set off by tram, then took the train to Ramsau. There, we squashed into a taxi to drive on to the holiday hotel. By the time we arrived, it was dark and we were exhausted and hungry. The owner offered us hot soup and bread, which we gratefully tucked into before going to our rooms.

Grandmother took Dagmar into her bed. Harold and Osrid shared a small back room. I slept with Gertrude and baby Helmut. We tumbled thankfully into strange beds. There was not a sound from baby all night.

Daylight revealed wonderful, breath-taking scenery. Austria`s second largest mountain, Dachstein, rose majestically above us.   The mountain seemed like a sentry and guardian. Sunlight sparkled on the snow at its peak; shadowed swards of green swept around the base. I opened the balcony window. Cool, clear air drifted in.

"Thank God," I breathed, then set about organising the day.

We had to register with the local council as refugees from the city. Our ration books were altered for the hotel to use. The boys could attend the local village school Everything seemed to fit into place easily.

"I feel we are in the hands of God," Grandmother said that evening.

"We are certainly living in a heavenly place," I agreed.

By the end of the week, I had had time to write letters to Frau List, to Annie, home to Mother, to Sister Alphana, and to my Josef, somewhere at the Front.

The children were exceedingly well-behaved. Other guests remarked on their demeanour and politeness. I felt very proud of them. I knew Harold and Osrid hated having to go to a new, very different kind of school, but they did not complain. I did though, when they came back with nits and I had to scrounge paraffin to douse their hair in the communal bathroom. The owner complained of the smell. I complained about hygiene.

Three weeks later, we woke to find the hotel foyer crowded with refugees from Yugoslavia, looking shaken and worn-out.

"We need your rooms," the owner told me.

"Where are we to go?" I asked.

"Speak to the council. Go down to the village now. They ordered me to take these people in, they can organise this mess."

I left Grandmother and the children sitting on packed bags in my bedroom.

"You will have to move out," said the council official. "The government has ordered it."

"But where to?"

"How many are you?"

"One old lady, five children and me."

He thought for a minute. "You could use a summer villa. It`s high in the mountain. Three bedrooms, one big living area and a cellar. No bathroom though. My friend lets it out to tourists."

"I`ll take it!"

"It`s very isolated."

"I`ll have it." I took a purse from my bag and started to count out money.

"You`ll need a pony cart to take you up there."

"Fine. We`ll go today. Please arrange it now."

The landowner came into the office, took a deposit and handed me the keys.

"I`ll be up next week. Do you think you will be all right up there?"

"Yes," I said. "Don`t worry. I grew up in the mountains."

He laughed. "I`ll say no more. Good luck!"

The wooden villa stood tucked into the side of the mountain. Its roof slanted steeply, a chimney pot to one side. The windows looked bare and dirty. The garden had been turned into a vegetable patch. We heaved our luggage up the gravel pathway to the front door.

"Here is the key to the kingdom," I solemnly announced, opening the door.

Our boots clattered on the wooden floor as we stood in the hallway and looked around. A large room, with an enormous wooden table, several chairs, one leather settee and a huge dresser, took up most of the space. A round iron stove, filled with logs, jutted into the room.

Off to one side was a small kitchen with an electric cooker, and more cupboards stacked with pots and pans. A stone sink, with one tap, was placed under the back window. I rubbed a patch in the dusty glass. The view was stunning. Ground fell away in green hillocks that overlooked a deep valley, with mountains rising behind.

I heard the children climbing the open staircase and went up after them. Three small bedrooms, with sloping ceilings under the eaves, each held a double bed. We found bedding and a spare mattress in the cupboard under the rafters, and settled who was to sleep where.

Meanwhile, Grandmother was inspecting the crockery in the cupboards and on the dresser. Helmut gurgled happily on the settee.

"I`ll start a cookpot," Grandmother called out.

We came down to find she had already lit the iron stove and was sorting through saucepans for a suitable pot. We unpacked rice and barley bags from the suitcase, which also held flour, sugar, coffee, raisins, dried milk for Helmut, and a brick of salt. Everything was set on the dresser.

In the kitchen, Grandmother selected a pan and turned on the tap to fill it. There was a shuddering, then clear mountain water spurted out.

"Shall I see if there are carrots in the garden?" suggested Harold.

"That`s stealing," said Osrid.

"One or two carrots? Don`t be silly!" retorted Harold.

"See if there`s an onion," I called after him.

"There`s an outside door here, under the house," shouted Harold. "I think it`s the cellar, but I can`t open it."

I went out to look. Logs were stacked either side of a thick wooden door. I tried the front door key, which fitted and turned in the lock.

Harold and I entered the dank storeroom. Sacks of potatoes were piled against one wall. There were shelves with empty jars and wine racks.

A huge metal wash-basin stood beside a copper boiler. In the far corner, an ancient stone oven, like the one in my own farmhouse, was blackened by neglect.

"I'm beginning to feel at home," I laughed.

Outside, a small alcove concealed an organic toilet.

"I think this is the bathroom," I said.

"You mean we have to go outside?" said Harold in disgust.

"I had to," I replied.

Next afternoon, Grandmother rested in her room with Helmut and Gertrude. Outside, the children raced around the grounds, screaming with pleasure at the space and freedom. I called to them to come in and sit on the settee.

"Look, I'm on my own with you lot. That means I have to do the cooking, baking, cleaning, washing, shopping, everything."

They looked sheepish.

"So you must take on some chores. I expect you to make your beds as usual, clean your shoes, help with the cleaning and clearing up, and do the washing up."

"I can't reach the sink," said Dagmar.

"You can on a chair," said Osrid.

"None of you must handle the kettle with hot water," I warned. "I will fill the sink, you can do the rest. All right?"

"What about school?" asked Harold.

"You can return to the village school next Monday."

"But it's miles away. It will take an hour to walk there!"

"I had to do it," I repeated.

14 ORION

(February 1943)

The temperature was icy. Frost laced the windows. Air felt like sharp knives in our lungs. I heated bricks in the fire, wrapped them in towels and slid them into our beds at night. We snuggled up together to keep warm.

During the day, Grandmother found going about too much. She sat by the fireside trying to keep warm, wrapped in a blanket. The children watched eagerly as snow fell along the ridges and winds swept it against the little villa.

"Can we go out to play?" nagged Osrid.

"It's too dangerous," I said. "You'll be turned into a snowman yourself."

We were completely housebound, aware of nothing beyond our snowy patch and the occasional sun glow on the mountain tops. I longed to hear from Josef. When I looked at the stars, I sent him my thoughts.

It seemed weeks before the weather cleared enough to get down to the village. Harold and I skied down with haversacks on our backs to collect provisions. We were only able to get rations of flour and lard, some cheese and milk. The shopkeeper laughed when I asked for sausage-worsht.

At the post office, we sent off our long letters. There were two waiting for us. One from Josef, saying little except words of love, which I kept to myself. Grandmother read aloud her letter from Frau List. Annie had returned home so she was left alone with Aunt to do everything herself. She was very put out.

"She should be here," Grandmother said, rocking with laughter.

We had not been able to glean much in the village about the progress of the war. No one was allowed to own a wireless. Anybody found to have one would be shot. There were no newspapers. Food shortages preoccupied everyone.

Just before Christmas, the villa owner had arrived with helpers to remove his sacks of potatoes. I paid him to leave us one sack of potatoes and another of turnips and onions. Now, we were out of meat and eggs, with no chance of getting any more. We were living on vegetable soup, and bread that I managed to bake in the stone oven.

One evening, as I put the loaves to cool by the sacks of vegetables, I noticed a door that had been hidden behind the original pile. It squeaked open onto a narrow staircase leading into the house.

"We could have used this all the time," I thought. "But where is the door upstairs?"

Back in the living room, I discovered it behind the dresser.

"How strange," I thought.

I went back outside to collect the bread, lit a candle and tried ascending the little staircase. A small alcove, halfway up, revealed a wireless set. There was a cable running from the back that would fit into the electric cellar light. I tentatively switched it on. After a great deal of cracking and static buzzing, I heard a newsreader speaking in German. I listened intently, and in secret, to the progress of the War.

The siege of Stalingrad was over. The German Sixth Army had surrendered to the Russians. Ninety one thousand German troops had been taken into captivity. My mind was in turmoil. Was Josef one of them? I wanted the war to end soon and destroy the Nazi regime in Germany, before we were all destroyed.

After the transmission, I heard a drum play *dot, dot, dot, dash,* which was the signal used by the BBC, broadcasting to occupied Europe. I crept back to bed with a heavy heart. I prayed that Josef should be safe, that soon everything would get back to normal, so that we could begin our married life together, at last.

In the meantime, the children would be pleased to use the inside staircase, but they must never know about the radio. I had to disguise it somehow.

I covered it with a white cloth, set my crucifix on top and placed a prayer-card to the Virgin Mary in front.

"This is my own private chapel," I told them next morning, when I revealed the hidden staircase. "Someone has to pray for peace."

(March 1943)

From my bedroom window, I could see the clear, night sky, filled with stars. The same stars that looked down on my family in Neustift; on Josef, so far away. On a world at war.

"Auntie Mina, are you going to say your prayers?" Gertrude stirred sleepily, as I left her in my bed.

My nightly vigil by the wireless told me all I needed to know. Everyone was in danger in this war. My family, my brothers, my friends, my employers, my beloved Josef.

Helmut was grizzling when I crept back into the bedroom. His head was hot and he was very thirsty. By the morning he was burning up.

"I'm going to have to get him to a doctor," I said. "Harold, help me get him into this haversack on my back."

We strapped the baby in as securely as possible and I set off skiing down the slopes to the village.

"He has measles," said the doctor. "Keep him cool, plenty of fluids. There`s not much more you can do. Keep the other children away or they will catch it."

By the time the snows were melting, Harold and Osrid, Dagmar and Gertrude, had gone down with it, one after the other. Grandmother and I nursed them with cool cloths on their foreheads. We dabbed water on their reddened limbs. Even the soles of their feet were covered in the rash. They were stoic in their illness.

"I`m very sorry I can`t help you," murmured Harold through his fever.

"I`ll try to be specially good when I`m better," said Osrid, as I sponged him down.

"I do love you, Auntie Mina," said Dagmar, holding my hand limply.

"Will you stay, always?" asked Gertrude, as I cuddled her to sleep."

Grandmother helped as best she could, but she was getting frail and needed lots of rest. By the time Spring arrived, the children had regained their health and energy, but Grandmother seemed to find even walking an effort.

Food stocks were getting seriously low. I wrote to Frau List to relieve me of my duties for a week. She arrived on the owner's pony and cart three weeks later.

Before I set off, the girls clung to me.

"Don't leave us," cried Gertrude and Dagmar.

"I'll be back, you'll see," I said.

"Promise?"

"Of course."

I felt strangely alone on my way to the station. My ticket took me to Sebersdorf. I walked to Neustift and trudged the hill road to our farm. Hedwig saw me first and called for Mother to come out.

"Mina's home!" she yelled .

Mother, with her baking apron on as always, took my face in her hands. She looked worn out.

"Come inside," she said.

"How are the boys? How's Wigel? Have you heard from Maria and Josephine?   Where's Anna?"

"Sit down, I'll give you the news. Joseph is in Germany and writes he is well. All the girls are fine. But Alois," she paused and wiped a single tear away. "He was killed..last week...in Russia."

We wept together. Too many boys were dying in this awful war. What was it all for?

My suitcase was packed, heavy with food. Mother had spared cheese, butter, flour and lard. In the village, I had bargained for some black-market veal and sausages. I helped myself to two jars of blackberry and apple jam.

"This takes me back," I smiled.

The train to Ramsau was crowded with many wounded soldiers, on their way to the mountains to convalesce. Several whistled as I got off.

"Hi, sweetheart! Give us a kiss!"

Two letters from Josef waited for me at the post office. I put them in my coat-pocket to read later, and made my way back to the villa.

"Mina`s home!" yelled the children, as they saw me coming from a distance.

"Thank goodness you`re back! They`ve quite exhausted me," said Frau List, packing her bag.

With the replenished larder I made fresh bread and puddings, cakes and biscuits, enough to last.

"Does your Josef know you`re a good cook?" asked Osrid, helping himself to a biscuit.

"I don`t suppose he does."

"Why don`t you send him some biscuits, then he`ll know."

I laughed. "They would break in the envelope."

"No, they wouldn`t. You can use my special tin pencil box," he said, running upstairs to fetch it.

We packed the biscuits tightly into the tin, with a note from me and a drawing from Osrid. Then we wrapped it with brown paper and string, and took it down to the post office together.

"That should reach him in a week or so," I told Osrid. "Do you think he will love me when he tastes them?"

"Sure to," said Osrid.

Grandmother was waiting for us in the garden. She seemed almost sprightly.

"Someone's in your room," she said to me.

My heart sank. Something had happened to Josef. I flew upstairs and stood in the doorway. My darling Josef was standing in my bedroom, waiting for me. I flung myself into his arms.

"Ouch!" he said, gently pushing me away.

"Josef! You're wounded!"

"I'm all right. It's nothing, just my shoulder. Don't cry."

"But I've just sent you biscuits." I was laughing and crying together.

We went downstairs to where Grandmother sat, surrounded by the children, all anxiously waiting.

"Are you going away again?" asked Osrid.

"No, of course not. Josef is convalescing near here."

"But I should like to take her out tonight - if that's all right with you?" he requested.

We were a happy family that day. Josef sat with Harold and Osrid telling them his tales, while Gertrude helped me to prepare a good lunch. Grandmother, Dagmar and baby Helmut walked around the vegetable patch looking for caterpillars.

"A wonderful lunch, Hermione," said Josef, patting his stomach.

"She`s a good cook, isn`t she?" said Osrid.

That evening, Josef and I sat side by side in the local hotel, drinking coffee, talking about the war.

"Everything`s a mess out there." His eyes looked into the distance as if he could see the battle. "We may not have much of a future, Mina, my dear, but I want you to be my wife."

"We hardly know each other," I said, with his arm around me.

"We know we love each other," he said.

"How do I know we`ll be happy together?" I thought of the rows Mother had with Wigel over money.

"You`re my girl," said Josef. "That`s enough."

"I`m not a girl," I pouted. "I`m twenty three."

"You are to me," he laughed. "I`m ten years older than you!"

"Marry me! Marry me!" sang Dagmar in the garden after we announced our plans.

"Can we come to your wedding?" asked Harold.

"No, dears."

"Why not?" said Gertrude. "I want to be your bridesmaid." She held out her skirt and twirled round.

"The wedding will be a long way from here. In Eger. If it`s still wartime, none of my family will be there." I squeezed Josef`s hand. "Only Josef." I added.

Warmth and love surrounded me, more than I had ever imagined. Josef came daily to spend time with us. Just having him around was enough to make the days carefree.

Evening had darkened the land and the stars were twinkling when he stood at the gate with his arms around me.

"I return to my regiment tomorrow."

"No!" I cried.

"Look up there." He pointed to the stars. "They`ll be our messengers."

I could not see anything for tears.

"See Orion?" I nodded, though I did not look up.

"He stands guard over us. Look, see his belt? Three bright stars in line, holding him together. See them?"

This time I looked up to the heavens and followed where Josef was pointing.

This time I could see. Amongst the myriad of twinkling lights, Orion`s belt was clearly visible.

Josef spun me round and took my face in his hands.

"We`ll send messages with Orion. All right?"

I nodded.

"Every evening, at eleven, look for him and see him standing firm."

"How will we send messages?" I was too distraught to take much in.

"If he stands intact, we`ll know we are safe."

"And...?"

"If the stars on his belt are not intact, we`ll know something has happened."

"Josef!"

"I'll get a message to you somehow, if anything does happen." He kissed me tenderly. "My dear girl, don't worry. I do love you."

"Write twice a week." I clung to him, not wanting him to go.

"Of course." He gently held me away. "I`ll think of you every minute though."

He turned and strode downhill, turning every now and then until he was hidden by the dark.

"I love you!" I called into the blackness.

15 THE WEDDING

(Summer 1943)
Every letter I received from Josef was like a
precious jewel. I hid them in my treasure box,
with my bible. Sometimes they came regularly,
sometimes as many as eleven in one go. Now
that the children knew him better, they made
pictures and sent little messages to him with
mine.

As the days grew hotter, we spent more time
outside, climbing the base of the mountain and
exploring the forest.   While the boys were at
school, I took the little ones into the fields to
collect wild flowers.

"Let's sunbathe," I said. "Come on, off with
your clothes."

"All of them?" asked Dagmar.

"Fresh air and sunshine will do you the world
of good."

"You too," Dagmar insisted.

We lay on a blanket soaking up the sun. Planes
droned   above,   circling in the blue sky.
Suddenly, one came down lower and flew back
over us with dipped wings. We could see the
pilot giving a `thumbs up`. I grabbed hold of the
children and pulled them into the cover of some
trees where we ducked down, waiting for the
sound of the engine to fade away.

113

"What a cheek!" I exclaimed.

"He saw us with nothing on," said Dagmar, indignantly.

"It`s happened before," I giggled.

Grandmother rocked with laughter when we told her.

Towards the end of July, Josef wrote saying he had arranged three weeks leave at the beginning of September. Did I still love him enough to marry him? I was overjoyed. This was one letter I could not keep secret and I rushed to Grandmother.

"I`m going to marry him, whatever happens," I said, hardly believing it to be true.

"Of course, my dear. Write to my daughter-in-law. She will relieve you of your duties, I`m sure."

There was so much to organise. Letters to Josef, letters home to Mother and Wigel, letters to Frau List in Graz, letters to Maria in Vienna, to Sister Alphana at the convent, letters to my new family-to-be in Eger.

"We are planning this like a military operation," I wrote to Josef.

He wrote back, "It is!"

"Good Luck!" shouted Grandmother, Frau List and the children as I turned to wave on my way down to the station in the valley.

I stuck my head out of the compartment window as the steam train chugged into Graz station.

"Josef!" He stood waiting on the platform, a soldier in uniform, holding a bunch of flowers.

Aunt welcomed us into the big house.

"You are staying tonight," she said, "So I have arranged a good meal for you. Do you mind eating it in the kitchen? I'm the only one here now."

The house was uncannily quiet. We crept up to my bedroom after supper and lay on the double bed, hugging, kissing and laughing together.

"We're meant for each other," said Josef.

"Can we have a very large family?" I asked.

"After we are married," he replied, "And only when the war is over."

"Josef!"

"These are not happy days for families. Better times will come."

Next morning, Aunt handed me a large cardboard box, tied with ribbon.

"This is for you from the List family," she said. "Josef, please leave the room!"

I opened the box gingerly and drew in a deep breath of joy. Inside was a pure silk wedding dress, specially made for me by a dressmaker. I lifted it out carefully. Underneath was a diamante head-dress and flowing veil. It suddenly reminded me of my confirmation day all those years ago.

"You will make a beautiful bride," said Aunt, kissing my cheek.

Next morning, Josef and I took the steam-train to Sebersdorf. I shared all my childhood memories with him as we walked towards Neustift and our farmhouse. Wigel, Hedwig and Anna were in the fields gathering the harvest, but Mother ran out across the farmyard to embrace us both.

That evening I introduced my husband-to-be to our neighbours and friends.

"He`s gorgeous!" said Josephine.

"Does he have a brother?" asked Hedwig, who had grown into a beautiful teenager.

"A brother and a sister, but you`re too young, so sorry for you!" I teased.

Maria had made a special journey to be with us. Her wedding gift was six bottles of the best wine for our reception. Everyone showered us with good wishes. All the gifts were edible! Our bags and suitcases were stuffed with food. Flour, eggs, sugar, fat, butter, enough to make a dozen cakes, as well as ham, sausage worsht and sauerkraut.

We struggled to lift them onto the train the next morning, on our way to the north and Eger.

We arrived exhausted from the long journey. Josef's sister, who was also called Maria, stood in the hallway of the Bohm house, smiling happily at us. Her mother embraced Josef and then hugged me like a long-lost daughter.

"Hermione, just as I imagined from Josef's letters." Mrs. Bohm beamed at her son. "You are right, she is lovely! Lucky boy!"

"I'm the lucky one, Mrs. Bohm," I said.

"No, you must call me 'Mother'. You are family now."

"Not quite," laughed Josef. "Not until I've made her tie the knot."

After the provisions were unpacked on to the kitchen table, Josef took me to his bedroom.

"My room is your room," he bowed me in.

"Where will you sleep?"

"At uncle's, just round the corner...'till we're married!"

We stood for a while looking out of the window, with our arms round each other, thinking of our past and our future together.

Very early next morning, when I arose, Mrs. Bohm was already in the kitchen beating eggs for cake making.

"Do let me help," I offered.

"Certainly not! I enjoy making cakes too much. Besides, it is your wedding tomorrow. Off you go with Josef, to meet the family."

Most of Josef's cousins were conscripted into the army, but he took me to see his uncles and aunts, who welcomed me warmly.

"All set for tomorrow?" asked an uncle. "Got the ring?"

"Of course," said Josef calmly. "Everything is arranged. The Registry Office at eleven. Church at two. The reception at my house. And by the look of it, enough food to feed an army!"

"My goodness!" I suddenly remembered. "I don't have a bouquet!"

We dashed to the florist, who promised to make me the best bouquet she could.

"Now, you haven't forgotten anything else?" teased Josef.

"Like what?"

"A nightie?"

"Really!" I blushed. I loved him dearly but he was, after all, the first boyfriend I had ever known. Being married, belonging to each other, was an enormous step.

(11th September 1943)

My wedding day dawned fair and warm. I stretched out in Josef's double bed, in the room he had grown up in, surrounded by his books, trophies and treasures.

"If every day is as bright as this," I thought, "I shall be happy all my life."

118

Josef called round for me at ten-thirty. Josef's mother, his sister Maria, and I had been busy organising the room for the reception, setting out the food and drinks.

"Well, you certainly look as if you belong here," said Josef, kissing me.

"I do," I agreed.

The four of us walked to the Registry Office for the short, civil ceremony demanded by law. I did not feel very married on the way back, but I kept twisting the ring on my finger, just to make sure it was there.

"Now, Mrs. Bohm," said Josef at the door of his home, "Please return my ring."

I twisted it off and dropped it in his palm.

"We're not married until God says we are," I agreed.

"See you at the church, then. Until then, I am abandoning you!" He kissed me hard on my lips, then walked back to his uncle's house.

In his bedroom, I lay daydreaming until it was time to get ready. Maria helped me slip into my beautiful, cream wedding dress. I sat on his bed as she pinned the diamante head-dress and veil on my head. In the mirror, Cinderella was transforming into a princess.

Several friends and relations were waiting at the foot of the stairs to applaud as I floated downstairs. Josef's sister handed me my bouquet of white carnations, then we stepped into the sunshine to walk to church. All along the church pathway, kindly onlookers threw rose petals at my feet, so that I walked upon a flowered carpet to my wedding.

At the church gate, Josef's uncle was waiting to give me away. The organ played as he walked me up the aisle to where Josef, with his brother as best man, stood waiting. I glanced shyly at my good-looking, blue-eyed soldier, who loved me enough to want me beside him for the rest of his life.

"Do you take this woman, Hermione Kohl, to be your wife, in the sight of God and this holy congregation?" intoned the priest.

"I do," said Josef, confidently. He looked immaculate in his uniform.

"Do you take this man, Josef Bohm, to be your husband, in the sight of God and this holy congregation?"

"I do," I said.

We knelt to take the sacrament together.

"God has brought me to this happy moment," I thought, more in a dream than I had ever been.

"You may kiss the bride."

I was gathered into the arms of my husband and kissed, in front of everybody! Then he tucked my hand into his arm and walked me down the aisle, with the organ playing joyfully.

We came out into the sunlight where his battalion friends stood guard of honour, their swords held high to make an archway for us. We were showered with flower petals and someone pushed a horseshoe into my hand.

A photographer stepped forward while everyone around cheered and shouted their good wishes in the sunshine.

I realised then that I held a gloriously happy moment in a dark world. A silent tear coursed down my cheek, which I quickly brushed away with the back of my hand. My husband put his arm around my waist and pulled me to him as if he would never let me go. Then, holding hands and laughing, we made our way back to the house for an evening of revelry.

Despite all the restrictions of the war and shortages of food, the tables at home were laden. A friend with an accordion played Austrian music whilst we chatted merrily and drank toasts to each other. The atmosphere was warm and jolly, even though it was not a bit like the huge reception my sister, Maria, had enjoyed. I missed her and all my family.

I was really a stranger in a strange town, living with people I barely knew, and yet I felt truly at home and part of the Bohm family.

The merrymaking went on until midnight, when the guests suggested laughingly and loudly that Josef should take me up to bed.

We disappeared into his bedroom and closed the door with a bang. Then we sat on the bed, whispering to each other.

"They're outside listening!" said Josef, putting a finger on my lips.

"What for?"

"Us! Come here, let me unzip you. Tiptoe round the bed and lie beside me."

He undressed and lay quietly under the covers, gazing at the ceiling, as I crept into bed and lay in his arms. We could hear giggling outside on the landing.

"Goodnight, Mrs. Bohm," said Josef, kissing my forehead. And we both promptly fell fast asleep.

We made love in the early hours of the morning, when we were refreshed and close to each other, and the house was silent and still.

Several guests had stayed the night because of hangovers. They looked curiously at us when we came down to breakfast.

"Well?" said one.

"Well what?" queried Josef.

122

"You were very quiet last night. Did anything happen?"

Josef laughed, "That`s for us to know and you to guess."

"Not much of a night then," said his uncle. "The bed stayed on the brick."

"What?" roared Josef.

"We tipped the bed on a brick, so it would fall as you jumped on it!"

Mother Bohm laughed.

"You can`t catch out such innocents," she chuckled, shaking her finger at her brother. "Not everyone is as randy as you!"

I was horrified that they had tried to listen to our privacy, but I had to make the best of it and pretend I did not mind.

We spent the next week living contentedly together in Josef`s home, being looked after by his mother and sister. Many of Josef`s friends and relations came to visit and wish us `Good Luck!`. From now on, my life was going to be different. I knew that I felt different. I wanted it to go on forever.

"You will see me off in the morning, like a good girl, without crying," said Josef, in bed that night.

But I could not stop the tears, through the night, or on the platform, as I hugged him goodbye.

"Remember Orion," he whispered in my ear. "Eleven every night, we will look to see him standing firm."

"If anything does happen?"

"Then we will know because his stars will disappear."

"For God's sake, take care," I cried. "And write to me every day."

The whistle sounded as the huge engine began to gather steam. The carriages jerked forward, stopped, then slid slowly onwards, behind the steam giant that pulled my love away from my arms.

16 BAD NEWS

(Christmas 1943)
There was little to rejoice about. I twisted the golden ring on my finger, longing for Josef. Outside, snowdrifts like bales of cotton wool wrapped around the villa. The wind howled continuously and blew into corners of rooms, twisting into icy draughts.

Grandmother was coughing badly and spent most of her time in bed. I kept her there with warm bricks at her feet and hot drinks on her bedside table. The children huddled near the stove, wearing extra knitted scarves, trying to keep cheerful by playing imaginary games about Santa Klaus, or singing carols. No letters got through the storm. No news filtered to our mountain, because reception on the hidden radio became so poor that I had stopped trying to pick up the stations.

Christmas dinner consisted of piping-hot potato soup, chunks of home-made corn bread smeared with butter, followed by a raisin cake I had made months before.

I skied down to the post office later in the week with my correspondence. Three letters from Josef were waiting for me, along with cards for the children from their parents, and several letters for Grandmother.

She was tucked in bed when I handed her letters over, with another hot drink. I went downstairs to help the children read their cards. My letters from Josef would have to wait.

Suddenly, I could hear Grandmother crying out. I rushed upstairs and found her prostrate on her pillow, sobbing her heart out.

"Whatever is it?" I soothed her, with my arms round her.

"Don`t tell the children," she whispered. "Don`t upset them now."

"What`s happened?"

"It`s Manfred. He`s dead." Grandmother pulled herself up, and held out a letter from her son.

I could hardly believe what I read. Professor List wrote that Manfred had been forced into the Hitler Youth movement. He had been bullied and beaten, made to run bare-foot over corn stubble. His father wrote that he knew of Manfred`s distress, but never realised the effect it was having. Manfred, who was a kind and sensitive boy, had eventually taken his mother`s gun from their home, walked to the banks of the Danube and shot himself.

There was nothing left to say. Manfred`s untimely death was the true evidence of the evil regime that had overpowered us. I sank to my knees by Grandmother`s bed, and we prayed for his dear soul to rest in peace. Neither of us mentioned the terrible news to the children.

(Spring 1944)
By the time the weather improved, we were running out of food again.

"This is no good," I said, helping Grandmother, who was unsteadily trying to get dressed. "I`m going to work."

"Whatever are you saying? Don`t you work enough here?`

"The boys attend school. Dagmar has started at nursery school. Could you look after Gertrude and Helmut, just for three hours?"

"Are you going to work at the school then?" asked Grandmother.

"No! At the farm, lower down the hill," I replied.

The farmer was finding it difficult to run the farm alone with his wife. The hired hands had all been called-up. He was happy to have my offer. We came to the arrangement that he would pay me with food, if I milked the cows and did general jobs.

After that time, milk, eggs, butter, cheese and yoghurt replenished our diet. Occasionally, meat or ham were on the table. Grandmother`s health improved. The children grew sturdy and strong.

But my days were so full, I barely had time to write a note to my husband.

Harold was growing tall very quickly. His ankles stuck out from the bottom of his trousers.

"I'm beginning to look like a clown!" he said.

"I'll see what I can do tonight," I promised.

That evening, when he was in bed, I cut strips from a grey blanket and sewed them on the bottom of his trousers to lengthen them.

"I expect he will think he looks even more ridiculous," I reflected, laying them at the foot of his bed before I went to sleep.

But he was genuinely pleased.

"Everyone's got patched up clothes at school," he told me.

(Summer 1944)

I worked on the farm, even at weekends. The children knew where I was if they needed me. Often, they would wander down to watch me milk the cows. They were growing up, and I felt they would come to no harm alone on our docile mountain-side for a while.

"Can I have a bucket, please?" Dagmar stood in the kitchen one Saturday afternoon, looking timid.

"Whatever for?"

"Something. Osrid said it's for a surprise."

She pulled the bucket after her. I watched as the children wandered off towards the forest with it.

"I bet they are going to gather berries for me," I thought happily.

I went into the cellar for empty jam jars to fill with home-made bilberry or blackberry jam. I washed them in soapy water, and left them to dry until the children returned. Helmut played in the garden, while I sat in the sun waiting for the children's harvest.

I could see them approaching up the green slopes. Harold was giving Gertrude a piggy-back. Osrid and Dagmar bounced up behind.

"What have you got for me?" I asked, as they came into the garden.

They looked at one another, puzzled.

"We've brought your bucket back," said Osrid.

"Well, thank you!" I was disappointed that it was empty. "Whatever did you want it for?"

Dagmar put her thumb in her mouth. Osrid hopped from one foot to the other, looking into the empty bucket. Harold set Gertrude down and stood silent. They seemed intent on not telling me.

"Come and have tea, you lot," I said. "I'll bring it out as a picnic, if you like."

This cheered them up. We ate outside on a blanket, with Grandmother sitting on an old wicker chair.

I suddenly realised we were being watched by a couple of soldiers who had wandered up the mountain-side. One had his head bandaged, the other used a walking-stick. They both looked worn-out with the effort of the climb.

"Do you want to join us?" I said, thinking of Josef.

Their faces lit up.

"Thank you," said one. "You don't know how wonderful it is to see a happy family together. I really miss my kids."

They spent half an hour or so sitting with us and chatting.

"Are you allowed to tell me where you were wounded?" I asked.

"Italy," said one.

"I don't suppose it matters too much if we tell you the Tommies and Amis have landed in Normandy," said the other.

"You mean, the British and Americans are on their way?" I said.

"What do you know about it?" one asked suspiciously.

"Nothing," I replied. "I just know I want the war over as quickly as possible. Then no more boys will die."

"Do you miss your soldier?" asked Osrid later, as I tucked him into bed.

"Of course I do."

I bent to kiss him goodnight.

"We weren't very naughty," he said.

I waited for an explanation.

Harold lay in bed next to him, staring at the ceiling.

Osrid took a deep breath. "I knew I could do it, and I could."

"Do what?"

"Milk cows, like you."

"Which cows?"

"The ones in the farmer's field, down the hill. I milked a cow and we all had a drink. No one saw us because we led her into the forest. So I know it is all right. Isn't it?" He paused and looked anxiously at me. "We took her back after."

"Really, Osrid," I said sternly, "That's stealing."

"From a cow?"

"Well, I suppose she had milk to spare," I laughed. "We'll say no more about it."

But I thought 'Growing children need milk.' I turned a blind eye when the bucket was borrowed again. They were obviously hungry.

Food was becoming scarce. Mother wrote that the Germans had commandeered all the produce of our farm and there was precious little left.

Certainly my farmer had little produce to pay me with. We had not eaten cheese or meat for months. Our area was being used for field hospitals, filled with wounded soldiers. There was also a prisoner of war camp lower down.

"I'm going to take our ration books to Schlagmink tonight," I told Grandmother, one Friday afternoon. "There's more chance of buying meat in a town than in our village. I'll be back tomorrow. Can you manage till then?"

After the children were in bed, I left for the town. The late train arrived in Schlagmink by ten thirty. Several skiing hotels were still open, so I took a room for the night in the one nearest the station.

"Are you in town for long?" asked the owner.

"Just for shopping," I said. "I have five children and an elderly lady to feed in Ramsau. There's nothing to be had in the village, so I've come into town."

"If you want a butcher, go to my brother-in-law's shop," directed the owner. "But you'll have to get up early and be ready to queue."

"Could you wake me in time?" I asked, knowing that as soon as my head touched the pillow I would sleep deeply. I flopped onto the bed and was out.

A loud knock at the door made me jump into consciousness. It was still dark outside.

"Ready to get up?` asked the owner. "I`ve brought you a cup of tea."

I looked at the grandfather clock as I passed it on the stairs. It said three thirty.

The queue was already forming when I arrived. Several women, almost asleep, stood holding empty baskets and bags. No one spoke. We stood watching the sky lighten, listening to the dawn chorus. Eventually, a van arrived and the butcher opened up

It was worth the wait. I bought good rations of beef for all of us.

"You`re not from around here?" said the butcher, wrapping it up in paper.

"No, from Ramsau."

"That`s a way. Better make it worth your while. Want some pork sausages?"

Did I!

"Want some lard?"

"Hey! Karl, just because she`s got a pretty face!" grumbled someone in the queue.

My bag was heavy with food as I made my way to the station to catch the six o`clock Saturday morning train. I trudged the two and a half hour walk up the mountainside to the villa feeling very pleased with myself. I spent the time working out recipes for pies and dishes to keep us going.

The children ran down the slopes to greet me as I climbed towards them. When we turned through the gate, the owner of the villa stood up from the vegetable patch and shouted.

"I brought up the post. There's a letter for you."

After all my exertions, I had quite forgotten to visit the post-office.

There was so much to do that I had no time to open my letter from Eger until late into the evening. It brought bad news. Josef had been injured, his mother wrote. He was in a field hospital somewhere behind the lines. He would write when he could.

I cried bitterly, mainly because I could not nurse him better. I wanted so much to comfort him, but the never-ending war kept everyone apart. What was it all for? Why could we not live in peace and be happy?

I talked to Orion in the night, consoling myself that at least my husband was out of the fighting, and safe.

Josef's letter arrived two weeks later. He was convalescing at home in Eger, and would try to see me.

"But I have to go to him!" I cried to Grandmother.

"Of course you must."

There was no question of waiting. Suddenly, nothing else mattered. I was overwhelmed by the desire to be by his side.

I left next morning, after telephoning Frau List from the station to come immediately to take care of her children.

17 REUNION

Josef was resting on his bed, his right arm in a sling, when I burst in.

"My darling girl, what a surprise!" His pale face lit up as he held out his left hand to pull me to him. I lay beside him on the bed, feeling his nearness and warmth, knowing I was home.

"I'm not much of an invalid," he said, later in the evening.

"Enough to have you safely at home, for me." I smiled.

By the end of the week, Josef felt well enough to take me out to dine in a restaurant.

"You have certainly made me feel better!" he said. " Do you remember when we met?"

I laughed. "I was sinking!"

"So was I." Josef squeezed my hand across the table.

"I feel like we're a real married couple," I said.

"We're an old married couple! We've been married almost a year."

"But we have hardly been together and we're never alone," I said, sadly.

"We will be."

We sat silently, thinking of our future together, but not daring to say more.

Next morning, Josef walked me out of town.
Just like the List family, the Bohms owned a small-holding, where the family farmed produce for themselves. He unlocked the door of his garden house and we were alone at last!

There were no tears at the station when I waved him goodbye.

"I just have to report to my regiment, then I should get leave," said Josef, from the train. "We will be together again in no time. Go back to the children. I'll write soon."

I walked back to his house still feeling the closeness of his love. Mrs. Bohm was dabbing her eyes.

"I hate the war. When will it all be over?" she cried.

Frau List was overjoyed to have me back in the villa. I had only been gone three weeks, yet everything seemed neglected. The children were listless. Even Grandmother's morale was low.

"Come along!" I chivvied them. "We'll all go down to see the steam-trains, wave your mother off, then climb the mountain!"

I was so full of happiness and energy that they soon caught my mood and everyone's spirits revived.

At two in the morning I crept to the wireless and tuned to the BBC. The news was encouraging. The Allies were advancing. Soon the war would end and we could live in peace at last. Until then, food was scarce because the Germans were commandeering all our goods.

Next day, on my way down to work on the farm, I passed a couple of soldiers guarding Russian prisoners of war.

"Hi! Mina! What are you doing here?"

"Karl!" It was a boy from my own village. "What are you doing here?"

He slung his gun forward. "Guarding prisoners."

"Be careful, Karl, and be kind to them. You may find yourself in their hands soon! The war is almost over."

He laughed. "It can`t be too soon for me! "

(September 1944)
Josef's letters piled high in my treasure box. They were full of love and hope. Finally, one came to say he had ten days leave in Eger next month.
I had no qualms in informing Frau List. But this time I managed to leave enough cakes and cookies, stews and soups to make sure the children were well fed while I was gone.

"Now you have homework to do while I am away. Harold and Osrid, you can offer to help the farmer at weekends, in my place." I instructed. "Dagmar and Gertrude are to go to the village school, so Grandmother and my Lady will only have Helmut. And he is as good as gold."

I felt I had organised everything as well as I could, but the children clung to me and insisted on coming to the station to see me off. As I stepped into the carriage and waved goodbye, I felt as if I was being torn in two.

"You look as handsome as ever," I said, gazing into Josef's bright blue eyes.

"You look worn out!" he replied. "Come on, I'm taking you for a treat!"

We walked in the park where he hired a rowing boat.

"Jump in!"

He tried to manoeuvre the oars and winced.

"You're still in pain! Move over, I'll row," I insisted, wobbling along to change places.

"Is there anything you can't do?" he groaned.

"No. But there are things you won't let me do."

"Like?"

"Having a baby." I rested on the oars, pleading with him.

"Not in this world. Not now. This is not a happy time for children."

I thought of my charges, and in my heart I had to agree.

Later, in bed that night I said, "But we will, won't we?

Josef took me in his arms.

"My darling girl, who knows what the future holds?"

I sighed. He was too strong to persuade.

Mrs. Bohm was so contented to have us in her home, we could hear her singing in the kitchen.

"You children, go off and enjoy yourselves," she ordered.

We worked on the smallholding together, harvesting potatoes. Sometimes, we went out to a restaurant for coffee and cakes. Sometimes we walked in the park. The Indian summer bathed us in sunshine. We spent every second together, until it was time to part.

"Don't cry! " Josef said, as I sniffed up the tears. "I don't want to think of you spending your life crying for me. Now, be a good girl. I may not come back, but if I do, we will have a wonderful life together. Just pray for that!"

As the train steamed into the station he grabbed me round the waist and lifted me off my feet. Several of his soldier friends, who were embarking, cheered as he kissed me and jumped into the carriage after them.

"Keep writing!" I cried.

"You bet! And remember Orion. Every night at eleven."

"I love you!" I sobbed, as the engine gathered steam and pulled the carriages out of the station.

18 ENDINGS

(Christmas 1944)

Every night I crept down to the wireless set to hear news of the approaching Armies. The war had to finish quickly. So many boys were being killed needlessly. My life was bound up with Josef. He just had to survive, for me. I wrote that I could not live without him. His letter, which crossed mine as always, said that I was always in his thoughts.

In the mountains, we were making do as best we could with our food rations. I had saved enough flour, fat, raisins and sugar to bake a Christmas cake. I made token gifts for the children; flaxen dolls in hand-sewn dresses for the girls, a home-made cloth teddy-bear for Helmut, knitted gloves for the boys, all of which I hid under my bed until Christmas Eve.

Early in the day, there had been a loud knock on the door which made us all jump. It was the farmer carrying a whole carcass of veal. The children cried to see it was a dead calf, but Grandmother and I got busy with preserving jars and cooking pans to give us enough meat to last the winter.

There was a smattering of snowflakes on Christmas Eve as I tucked the children in bed. We ate roast veal for Christmas lunch, which the children enjoyed, despite themselves.

(January 1945)
The weather suddenly worsened. Snow clouds hung across the night sky, so that the stars were hidden. Gales whipped up snow and sleet into flurries of cloud. We were immured in our little house, untouched by the war. No callers came, and no letters got through the snow. We kept our spirits up by drawing pictures, telling stories and singing carols around the stove.

My sleep was often broken. I usually rose in the night to listen to the wireless. Sometimes the children called for me, or Grandmother needed me. Always, I prayed for Josef.

Three weeks after Christmas, during the night, I heard his voice clearly saying, "My dear girl, I do love you!"

I woke with a start to see him standing by my bed smiling down at me.

"Josef!" I was overjoyed.

I sprang up to take his hand, but there was no one there. I ran to the balcony and threw open the window. The clouds had dispersed. The stars twinkled above. My eyes scanned the heavens for Orion. When I found him, I saw that the middle star on his belt was missing.

I could hear myself crying out, "My husband is dead!".

Grandmother found me sobbing in the cold. She hushed the children back to their beds.

"Mina!" She was gently pulling me into the room. I sank to the floor in anguish. She cuddled me, rocking me like a baby until I quietened down.

"There, there," she crooned. "I know how you feel. He is thinking of you, that is all."

"He is dead," I moaned, and would not be comforted.

"It often happens," said Grandmother, after a while. "They come to you before they go."

"But maybe he is not dead, just wounded," I said.

"We will have to wait and see," said Grandmother, gathering her shawl. "Go back to bed. He may come again to tell you all is well."

But I lay through the dark night feeling utterly alone.

(March 1945)

There was no news from Josef or from Eger. The broadcasts said the Russians were advancing on Vienna. Everything was in turmoil. All we could do was wait for the end of the war.

Early one morning, before we were up, there was a bang at the door. As I ran downstairs, the door burst open. A soldier in German uniform swayed at the threshold, then sank to the ground.

"Help me!" He spoke with an Austrian accent.

"Are you wounded?"

He shook his head.

"Water. Food." He was completely exhausted.

Harold and Osrid appeared.

"Go back to bed," I said.

"No, we'll help," said Harold, fetching bread from the kitchen.

I handed over a cup of precious milk.

"Has the war stopped now?" asked Osrid.

The soldier shook his head. "We never wanted to fight in the first place," he said. "Now, we're fed up and hungry. I just want to get home."

"Where's home?" I asked.

"Near Ramsau."

"Do you remember the name of the priest?" I wanted to make sure he was not lying.

"Father Peter. He confirmed me," he said.

I gathered more news from him after he had slept. Many men were being taken prisoner as

145

the push towards Berlin accelerated. The Russians were sending them back into Russia. My heart leapt at the thought that Josef was probably amongst them. Prisoners of war would return when it was all over.

"I have to get home," he said. "I`m the only boy left. My two brothers were killed last year."

I thought of Alois, long gone, and my brothers, Joseph and Franz. Until now, Mother had always written that they were alive, but I knew of one local family that had lost all their nine sons. The war just had to end, and quickly.

(May 1945)

"It`s over!" I ran to hug Grandmother. We were both crying with relief. Germany had surrendered unconditionally. The countryside was crawling with American GIs.

I was hanging out washing, the children were playing in the garden, when a bunch of GI soldiers, in smartly pressed uniforms, wandered up to our mountain home. They peered over our fence and beamed.

"Gee, this scenery is just something!" one exclaimed, but the children did not understand English and stepped back nervously. One sergeant held out a bar of chocolate. That helped. The children crowded round curiously as I took it and thanked them in broken English.

From then on, we were stared at by GIs who had wanted to climb the mountain. Some had bread or chocolate, which they offered to us. One black GI brought us a tin of peaches. We could not converse much with each other except with nods and smiles, but they all seemed genuinely impressed with our countryside, waving their arms high and giving the thumbs up.

There was still no news from Josef. His mother wrote to say that I should go to her, to wait for him. I wanted that very much, but Professor List felt we should stay in the mountain until things settled down. Austria was being divided into four zones of occupation, Russian, British, French and American. Vienna was to be an international centre with divided suburbs.

It was not until July that we left the dear mountain that had sheltered us from the storms of war. The children were thrilled to be home at last. Annie had returned to her kitchen. A new housemaid was installed to look after the house.

Frau List called me to her room.

"Mina, you have done an incredible job with the children," she said. "We owe you a great deal. You know, you are quite a celebrity here. There has been a newspaper article about how you managed alone in the mountains. Here, look."

I was astonished to see my name in print.

"Have you heard anything of your husband?"

147

"No. Only that his mother has asked me to return to Eger to wait for him there."

"I think you deserve a rest. You look worn out," said my lady. "But don`t lose touch. You know you always have a home here, whenever you want to visit."

FINALE

Aftermath
(1945-1947)

19 HOSPITAL

The children came with Annie to Graz station to wave me off. Gertrude cried as I bent to hug her goodbye.

"I'll be back, don't you worry," I promised.

"We'll never forget you," declared Harold.

"I'll write to you every day," said Osrid. "You must write back to me."

"I'm used to writing letters," I laughed. "But you will have to share one between you."

Dagmar was silent.

"Shall I write you a special card?" I asked, as she burst into tears.

"Come on," I said. "You are almost grown-up now. The war is over. It is peace. Everyone is going to be happy."

"Good luck!" they yelled, as I stuck my head from the carriage window to get a last glimpse of them.

I sank into my seat by the window feeling exhausted as the train chugged towards my new home. It was overcrowded with passengers, many of them refugees and soldiers trying to get back to Czechoslovakia. I closed my eyes, grateful to have a seat near the window, and drifted into sleep.

On the rack above was my suitcase containing all I possessed in the world; my precious treasure box holding bundles of letters, my rosary and bible, my recipe book with Annie's dishes carefully noted, a few hand-sewn clothes and knitted stockings, a silk scarf which was a gift from Frau List, a picture book specially made for me by the children with drawings of our times in the mountains. My travelling visa and money were held tightly in my handbag, together with Josef's photograph and several of his letters. Annie had packed me some food and drink for the journey in a small basket which I placed under my seat.

Hours later, the train pulled into Hof, in Germany. We could hear a guard shouting "Everybody out!"

"But we have to get to Eger," everyone grumbled.

"That is in the Russian sector. Trains run no further than here,." advised the station master. "People from Eger are leaving for Austria today."

"What am I to do?" I lugged my suitcase down and stood on the platform, being jostled by angry passengers. "I have to find Frau Bohm."

"There's a train *from* Eger on the other platform now," said a porter.

The crowded carriages of that train held more refugees fleeing south.

"Does anyone know Frau Bohm?" I asked frantically.

"Frau Bohm's my neighbour. She's here somewhere," shouted a voice.

I could hear yelling down the line for "Frau Bohm". Suddenly, I saw my mother-in-law and Maria peering from an open window.

"It's me!" I yelled. I held up my arms to grab her hand.

"Mina!" screamed Josef's mother. "We're on our way to...."

Suddenly, my legs were giving way and everything was spinning around me. The last thing I remembered, before sinking to the ground, was that Josef would look after me now. I was falling away from the world into a quiet, white cloud.

Voices drifted into my unconscious mind, but I could not understand what they were saying. Sometimes I felt I was floating, sometimes I was being lifted or turned. I could sense movement around me. Water was held to my lips, but I could not drink. When I tried to move my arms, I could not lift them.

A German voice spoke quietly. "Are you awake?"

A doctor in uniform sat on my bed, taking my pulse. He wore a mask so that only his soft eyes looked down at me.

"Where am I?"

"In a field hospital in Halli."

"What happened?"

"You have typhoid. We`ve been quite worried about you."

"Where`s Josef?"

"I am Lieutenant Goldsmidt. What is your name?"

"Hermione. Frau Bohm. Josef is my husband."

"You`re married?"

I felt for my ring. It was gone.

"Where are my things?"

"You had nothing with you when they brought you in the ambulance."

I lay back exhausted, tears coursing down my cheeks. Everything gone, but I was too weak to protest.

"Because this is a field hospital, we are barrier nursing you. Do you know what that means?"

I nodded.

"Are you German?" I asked, not understanding who had saved me.

"I`m an American, in the US army," he said. "I grew up in Germany, a Jew, but I escaped the inferno. You have no idea what we are uncovering."

154

He stood up to leave, "Now, be a good girl and do what the nurses say."

I lay against white pillows, too weak even to raise my hand in thanks.

The barrier nursing kept me isolated from other patients and at the mercy of my nurses.

"We`ll have to get food into her," said a nurse in German, who was obviously not part of the US contingent.

"She won`t last the week," said her colleague.

They tried to get fluid into me, but I could not swallow. Eventually they rigged up a saline drip with huge needles. I was so thin they could not find a vein except in my neck, which hurt like hell. I cried so much they had to take the drip out.

"You must eat," they insisted, and tried to spoon porridge into me, but I turned my head away. One of them smacked me hard on the face in exasperation.

"I don`t know why we are bothering with you?" she said, sourly.

When Dr. Goldsmidt came to see me later, I had enough spirit to complain.

"She hit me because I did not eat the porridge!"

"Why didn`t you try?" he asked.

"At home we feed our pigs with porridge," I murmured indignantly. "I`m not a pig!"

155

They laughed, but Dr. Goldsmidt said, "We'll find you something more palatable."

After that I was fed with fortified drinks like blackcurrant or orange juices. They gave me vitamin pills, which I could not swallow. All my hair fell out. I weighed only forty-nine kilos.

Faces of curious men peered at me through the window in the bedroom door. Some gave me the thumbs up sign, or the victory sign. A small posy of flowers was placed by my bed to cheer me. The nurses had forgiven me for not eating porridge. They bathed and fed me, and tried to entice me to eat. Everyone was very kind, but I felt so ill I could barely respond.

I lapsed into unconsciousness again. Josef peered down at me. My father was shaking his head and Alois was calling "Mina!". I knew I was dying. I felt Josef lift me up and stand me on my feet. A great feeling of peace and love came over me. Jesus was there in all His glory, His arms open, His face smiling at me.

"She will not last the night. Take her into the bathroom."

As I was being lifted from the bed, I began to come to.

"I don't want to die yet," I murmured. "I have too much to do."

Dr. Goldsmidt's voice said firmly in German, "You have to fight to live. I know you can."

"I want to live," I sighed, and lapsed into unconsciousness again.

They nursed me so well, that by the end of the week I was able to sit up and take nourishment. My head was bald and I was thin as a stick. But the typhoid fever had gone and I was on the mend.

Gradually, with help, I was able to get out of bed. Dr. Goldsmidt stood by me as I looked down from the window of my room thinking how small people were on the ground.

"They are such tiny people," I exclaimed, "Are they a different race from us?"

"You're hallucinating," he said. "We're on the second floor."

I was puzzled. "Don't worry, your brain is not in order yet. But you will get better. Look at you! Last week you were at death's door."

"I'm here, thanks to you," I said.

But he was to have more problems with me. By the end of the month I had contracted pneumonia. My breathing rasped as I cried out. A huge pain dug into my side. I fell back on to the bed gasping for air. Injections of penicillin were administered into my frail body. I wanted to live. I just had to survive. I fought with medicine and prayer.

When eventually I began to take notice, I could see that my hands, my arms, all of me, had turned yellow.

"That's too much penicillin," I complained, feeling very sick indeed.

"You have jaundice now," said Dr. Goldsmidt, tutting over me. "You really are a naughty girl!"

One afternoon, when I was able to sit up in bed, a lady came to visit me.

"I've heard such a lot about you, Hermione," she said in German.

I looked curiously at her. She was very smartly dressed. Her accent was not one I recognised either.

She smiled. "I am Dr. Goldsmidt's wife." she explained.

"It's very kind of you to visit me," I said.

"Well, I have come with a purpose. We thought you might like to come to America with us."

"But I am Austrian."

"I know. But things look very bleak here. We want to give you a new start in the USA. Would you like that? We think you deserve it."

"I can't. I'm married," I said. "I have to wait here for my husband."

I burst into tears, sobbing, "I just want to go home."

"We`ll arrange something," she said, patting my hand.

I was too weak to travel alone.   An ambulance took me to Salzburg to convalesce for two weeks. Very gradually I gained my strength. My hair started to grow back. I was able to get to the bathroom on my own.

"Hi, young man!" someone called as I toddled down the corridor.

"I `m a married woman!" I said indignantly.

"Well, you could have fooled me!" he laughed.

By the end of two weeks, I was well enough to travel home. The Red Cross paid for a train ticket and gave me a little extra money. Apart from that, I had lost everything; my clothes, linen, wedding gifts, treasures, everything.

Wigel met me at the station with his cart. Mother wept when she saw how thin and ill I looked. Hedwig and Anna were there to hug and kiss me. We sat around the kitchen table exchanging news. Mother served up her special hot potato soup with freshly made bread and butter. It was the best meal I had had for years.

I slept soundly in my own bed that night, safe in the arms of my family once more.

Work on the farm had everyone up early. No one expected me to help, but over the next few weeks I managed to give a hand with the milking and baking.

My appetite returned. I was ravenous all the time. Mother was happy to feed me up and my figure began to return. Even so, I was not fully recovered. Suddenly, huge boils appeared all over my body. I found myself back in hospital again with septicaemia.

All my family, Maria, Josephine, Joseph, Franz, as well as Mother, Wigel, Hedwig and Anna, came in turns to Hapsburg hospital to visit me in my room. We talked over old times.

"I've lost everything I made for my trousseau," I said to Mother. "My wedding dress, all my presents, even my recipe book has been stolen. I've nothing at all left to remind me of the past."

"I thought that was so," she said, searching in her large handbag. "I've brought you the wedding photo you sent us."

I held it close, looking at darling Josef's face beside mine.

"Love never dies, my dear," said Mother, kissing me goodnight. "You have his love to remember, to carry you through. God bless you and keep you safe from any more harm."

Later, alone in the quiet of the night, I lay thinking of my future, probably without my husband. I was coming to terms with reality. I knew that working on a farm was not for me.

I owed my life to the skills and dedication of wonderful doctors and nurses. The vows taken so long ago at my confirmation were to dedicate myself to doing good. I realised then that I wanted to become a nurse.

20 ENGLAND

(Autumn 1946)

The minute I felt well enough, I rented a room in a boarding house in Graz. I was longing to see the children again, so I walked round to the List house as soon as I could. A new housekeeper opened the door. Frau List came to the top of the stairs to greet me. Grandmother stood behind her smiling broadly.

"Come and see who it is!" She called the children in from the garden.

They seemed shy of me. Harold stepped forward to shake my hand.

"You look different," said Dagmar.

"I've been ill."

"Why didn't you answer our letters? I did a special picture for you," Gertrude said accusingly.

"I knew you would come back," said Osrid, grabbing my hand to go outside where Helmut and his new nanny were playing. I hung back. I did not want to intrude.

"Is there any news of your husband? " asked Frau List.

I shook my head. "I've written to the Red Cross. They are doing all they can to trace him, but they believe his whole regiment was wiped out. I am probably a widow."

"It is so sad. So many boys killed," she said, wiping her eyes. "What are you going to do with your life now?"

"Well, I have to earn a living."

"Would you care to work as a housekeeper? The Haider family are my friends. They live nearby. They have grown up children, so you wouldn't have to nanny anyone. Would you like me to organise something?"

It was quickly arranged that I keep house for them all. I had my board and keep, but my wages were so little that I did not even have enough to spare for a pair of stockings.

Sister Alphana was concerned about me when I made my regular visit to her convent.

"You are working too hard again," she warned me.

"I'm getting stronger every day," I assured her.

"I think you should look for something better," she said. "I hear the British are advertising for auxiliary nurses to work in their hospitals. It would give you a new start."

"Is it worth trying for?"

"Apply, and if you get an interview, I will come with you," she said.

"To England?

"No, to speak on your behalf," she said. "I know you won't tell them half of what you can do."

(August 1947)

The preliminary interview was conducted in a local hall. A polite British soldier, who spoke German, took my details.

"We'll be in touch," he said.

The letter requesting me to report to the Field Hospital in Graz arrived in September. I wanted to look my best, so I wore a dress Frau List had given me; a pure silk, sleek, turquoise dress, with long sleeves, that hugged my figure.

"You look wonderful!" said Sister Alphana, as she waited with me in the corridor until we were shown into the medical officer's room. An English officer stood up from behind his desk as we entered and shook our hands.

"Please sit down. Do you speak English?"

I knew enough to say "No."

"I am afraid I do not speak German. Please let me get an interpreter."

He rose and gave orders to the soldier outside who entered, smiling at us.

"Why do you want a job in England?" they asked.

"I have to earn a living, "I said. "My husband did not return from the war. I am quite alone."

He seemed genuinely sad for me.

"Have you had any illnesses?"

"I nearly died from typhoid. I've also had pneumonia, jaundice and septicaemia," I said. "Apart from that, I'm fine!"

"You look very healthy to me," he said. "You must be a strong, young lady to survive all that."

"She is," said Sister Alphana, and promptly related to the interpreter all that I had done during the war.

"You're exactly what we are looking for," said the officer. "We just need to give you a medical. We can do that today. Oh, and you will need a passport to leave Austria."

I thought that the medical would be a problem and that getting the passport would be easy, but it turned out to be the other way around. I was pronounced fully fit by the medics. The Austrian government, however, were not prepared to release me.

I returned to the hospital to explain my position to the officer.

"I just don't know what to do!" I said. "I want more than anything to go to England, to be a nurse. I know that is my destiny. I just know."
I went on, "All the others are going, why can't I?"

"They want to keep their best workers here," he smiled. "Only refugees are leaving."

He turned over my papers and studied them.

"I see that your husband was from Eger in Sudetenland," he said.

"Yes, but I am a widow."

"Sudetenland does not officially exist any more," he continued. "As his wife, technically you are stateless."

"I am?" I was astonished.

"You can apply for "Stateless" documents. They will have to let you go."

"Thank you," I said, and thought, `Thank you darling Josef, for working it out for me!`

"We will give you a work permit. We will also pay your train and boat fare to get over there," said the British officer.

I shook my head. "No thank you. I will pay the fare there - but if I don't like it, you must pay for me to return to Austria."

"Done!" he said, shaking my hand and laughing.

I waited four weeks for all the papers to be approved and signed. Then I bade farewell to my godmother, who blessed me with the sign of the cross.

The List family held a dinner for me before I left. Professor List seemed the most envious of all that I was going to England.

It was a relief to be on dry land as we disembarked at Dover. Later, when I arrived at Victoria Station, two young soldiers were waiting for me with a placard saying "Hermione Bohm".

I stepped toward them.

"Welcome to Britain." They shook my hand. "Please come with us."

Because it was late in the evening, they took me to a local hospital to spend the night in a room of my own.

"Auf Wiedersehen!" one said next morning when I appeared for breakfast, which was porridge (which I ate!) and a cup of tea. They escorted me onto a train to the south of England, near Reigate, where we were taken by jeep to a small field hospital nearby.

At the hospital, everyone was very kind and considerate. I was issued with a nurse's outfit, then shown into my own bedroom. Matron introduced me to another Austrian auxiliary, so that we could talk to each other and not feel so lonely.

When I went on to the wards, the patients tried to speak German to me, making me laugh at their funny words and accents. Most of the words were wrong, but I did not mind. I was happy to be there, nursing the wounded.

Some of the boys helped me with my English, which eventually I learnt to speak, although I never lost my Austrian accent. However, I found I could read and write English quite well.

From that time on, I began to learn the art of nursing, which was to be my vocation for the rest of my life.

Opposite is the photograph of
Hermione and Josef Bohm
taken on their wedding day,
11th September, 1943

EPILOGUE

Hermione Bohm (Mina) came to England to look after war veterans, where she became a State-Registered Nurse. She never forsook Josef, but searched for him for twenty-five years through the Red Cross. She never married again.

She remained in England to specialise in nursing the elderly and infirm. Eventually, she set up her own, cosy nursing home for the aged.

Professor Dr. Hans List lived to celebrate his hundredth birthday. He was awarded an honorary doctorate at the University of Technology in Vienna.

(June 1997)
After fifty years of selfless work, Hermione Bohm left England for her own home in the Austrian mountains, near to the farmhouse where she was born. There she was reunited with her surviving sisters and her many nieces and nephews.

Historical background to events in the story.

1919-1926

After the 1st World War (1914-1918) the Hapsburg Empire, centred in Austria, collapsed. The Treaty of Versailles gave independence to Czechoslovakia and Hungary. The territory of Sudetenland was divided between Poland and Czechoslovakia, even though its people were German-speaking and had many ties with Austria and Germany. Austria became a Republic, its area much as it is today. The nobility lost their power, though many still owned land.

1927-1932

The depression was world wide. Financially, Austria was very weak. Constant financial collapses, leading to high inflation, led to general unrest in Vienna. There was fighting in the streets between the Government (Socialists) and Opposition (pro-German parties). Money lost its value. Often people were paid with suitcases filled with banknotes that barely bought the necessities of life. There were many beggars on the city streets. When crops failed in the countryside there was hunger everywhere.

1933-1935

In Germany, Hitler and Nazism came to power in January 1933. Austrians became divided into pro-Austrian or pro-German politics.

Many feared Communism. In Russia, the Tsar and all his family had been executed in 1918. Wealthy families there had everything confiscated. Many of them were murdered or fled into Austria.

1936-1937

The Olympic Games in Berlin added impetus to the health movement. People had became more health conscious. Sun clubs were formed to encourage improvement in personal health and fitness. Hiking, swimming and sunbathing were all the rage.

1938

(12 March 1938) The German invasion of Austria was called `Anschluss` (attachment). From then on, Austrian forces were incorporated into the German army to prepare for war. Many Austrians welcomed Anschluss, others did not approve of Germany`s actions.

(November 1938) In Germany, there were large-scale attacks on Jewish property (`Krystalnacht`). There were many wealthy Jewish families living in Vienna, some of whom decided to leave Austria. (See `Eva's Story`, a Survivor's tale by the step-sister of Anne Frank, published by Castle Kent).

1939

Germany invaded Poland in September. Britain declared war on Germany.
There were mounting shortages of food.
(See `The Disappearance of Goldie Rapaport`, published by Evelyn Kent)

1940

Most countries in Western Europe had fallen under German control. By the summer, Britain stood alone against Nazi Germany.

1941

(22nd June) Germany invaded Russia. Code name for this operation was `Barbarossa`. Believing it would be a short, successful campaign, large numbers of troops, without winter clothing, were sent to Russia, advancing easily at first. However, the Russians organised resistance, so that by winter German weapons

and transport became bogged down by snow
ice.

(7th December) After the bombing of Pearl
Harbour by the Japanese, USA entered the war.

1942
The Luftwaffe had failed to break Britain during
the Blitz. The RAF then began to bomb German-
held cities.

In German-occupied Yugoslavia, there was
resistance from General Tito and his partisans.

1943
In the severe Russian winter, the 6th German
Army under General Von Paulus surrendered to
the Russians at Stalingrad. It was the first defeat
of the German army during the Second World
War. The tide began to turn in favour of the
Allies. From then on the Germans were pushed
steadily back on the Russian front.

The Allies moved from North Africa and Sicily to
invade the mainland of Italy (3rd September)
British and U.S. troops landed near Naples,
advancing north towards Rome.

<u>1944</u>
(6th June) D-Day landing in Normandy took German troops by surprise. British, Free French and US soldiers pushed them back northwards, through France towards Belgium and Holland.
The Russians advanced from the East.

(20th July) Colonel von Stauffenberg and others wanted to end the war and make a negotiated peace with the Allies. However, their bomb plot to kill Hitler failed.

(25th August) Paris liberated.

(4th September) Brussels liberated.

<u>1945</u>
(11th April) Russian army entered Vienna after a seven day battle.
(13th April) Vienna liberated.
(5th May) US 3rd Army reach Karlsbad, east of Eger and other US units reach Linz in Austria.
(Midnight, 8th May) Guns cease firing in Europe. End of war with Germany

Hitler killed himself in the Fuhrerbunker in Berlin

Dr. Goebbels, Hitler's Minister of Propaganda, made sure his six children were given lethal injections before he and his wife killed themselves. Hermann Goering was captured and sentenced at Nuremberg to be hanged. He killed himself with poison.

Aftermath

Austria was divided into 4 zones of occupation - American, British, French and Russian. Identification papers were needed to travel between the zones. Eger was just inside the Russian sector. The town of Hof, in Germany, was in the American sector. Sudetenland was incorporated in the new Czech Republic.

The Austrian population suffered during the first winter after the war. There was little food or shelter. Relief agencies had not yet organised themselves to deal with so many refugees.

Major Norman Beynon-Davies (father of Michael Davies) served with the British Occupation forces in Graz. Since he spoke fluent German, he was frequently asked to interpret at interviews. He may even have met Hermione Bohm.

(Notes and commentary by Michael Davies, Historian in Twentieth Century European History)

also

Eva`s Story
(a survivor`s tale by the step-sister of
Anne Frank)
Eva Schloss and Evelyn Julia Kent
ISBN 0 9518865 09

`A patently honest account of the struggle of a
courageous and resourceful young woman to
survive in a nightmare world`

and

The Disappearance of Goldie Rapaport
Gina Schwarzmann and Evelyn Julia Kent
ISBN 0 9523716 26

`Goldie`s adventures are exciting and horrific.
There are moments when you have to cry, but out of
happiness too."